Tales of Old Buckinghamshire

Tales of Old Buckinghamshire

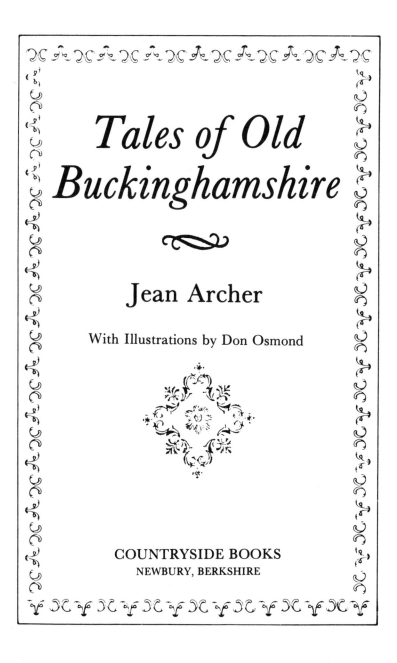

Jean Archer

With Illustrations by Don Osmond

COUNTRYSIDE BOOKS
NEWBURY, BERKSHIRE

First published 1987
© Jean Archer 1987
Reprinted 1988

All rights reserved. No reproduction
permitted without the prior permission
of the publishers:
COUNTRYSIDE BOOKS
3 CATHERINE ROAD
NEWBURY, BERKSHIRE

ISBN 1 85306 001 1

Produced through MRM Associates, Reading
Typeset by Acorn Bookwork, Salisbury
Printed in England by Borcombe Printers, Romsey

To Elsie King

Contents

CONTENTS

The Map overleaf is by John Speede and shows the county as it was in the early seventeenth century.

Leaps and Bounds
at
The White Hart

THE *White Hart Inn* at Aylesbury, which was demolished in 1864, was once considered one of the finest hostelries outside London and was an important centre in the life of the town. This was in the days when old Aylesbury was a quaint town of narrow passageways, nooks and crannies; a thriving County Town full of bustle and activity – the excitement of the hustings at election time, the bargaining of the cattle market and the gathering of the elite of the hunting and racing world. Situated next door to the Assizes, the *White Hart* was also frequented by barristers, solicitors and magistrates. It was a three-gabled building with a large gallery running around the great courtyard, a garden and a bowling green, and the courtyard was full of jostling post-boys, busy ostlers, grooms and chambermaids. Several of the large high-ceilinged rooms were named according to their function. The commercial room where the principal business of the town was transacted was called the Change Room, the Crown Room was where customs and taxes were collected and the Mitre Room where Church dues were paid.

J. K. Fowler was the proprietor and host in the middle of the last century and is revered and appreciated by local historians to this day. His great-grandfather had kept the

Crown at Amersham years before and his father, when he came of age, moved to Aylesbury and the *White Hart*. 'J.K.' was a friend to the many celebrated men from the political, sporting and agricultural worlds who frequented the Inn. A keen horseman himself, he was proud to know Lord Beaconsfield (Benjamin Disraeli), the Rothschilds, Lord Lonsdale, the Verneys of Claydon and Squire Drake from Shardeloes at Amersham. He died in 1902, but not before he had written three brilliant accounts of the gossip of the County including the goings on at the *White Hart*.

In 1835 friends in the hunting world sat talking of the steeplechase which took place every year at St Albans, and it was decided that Aylesbury should follow suit and run one that very year. One of the group undertook to lay out the course, which was to start from the windmill at Waddesdon (some four and a half miles from Aylesbury), with jumps across all kinds of fences and obstacles, including a lane, a brook, a spinney and, just for good measure, the River Thame which was all of 28 feet wide. The finish was to be the meadow before Aylesbury church. The course ran more or less alongside the turnpike road, thus enabling observers to watch the progress of the entire race.

On the morning of the race, crowds had gathered all along the road. The headquarters of the Race Committee was at the *White Hart*, which was packed with anybody and everybody from the hunting world. In those pre-railway days, people coming from London had to arrive the night before and all the rooms at every inn were taken, while to find stabling was impossible. Horses and riders weighed in at the *White Hart* – weight limit 12.7 lb, 20 guineas entrance fee and a 50 guinea silver cup for first prize.

The Aylesbury Steeplechase proved to be so popular that it became an annual event, drawing crowds from near and far each year. The after-race feasts were magnificent affairs and menus of great length were provided. In fact, Squire Drake of Amersham once gave a dinner to seventy gentlemen and just one of the courses consisted of 26 dishes of fish.

The younger members of the hunting fraternity could be

something of a nuisance to the *White Hart* innkeeper and J. K. Fowler recounts in his *Echoes of Old Country Life* how the young Marquis of Waterford (whose horse had died as a result of the race) was in the garden of the inn with two friends when, in order to impress, he hit on the idea of taking his horse up the steep steps into the dining room. This they considered hilarious and the three, who were obviously tipsy, led the horse around the table and refreshed it with apples and biscuits.

However, manipulating the horse back down the steps was a different matter and wiped the smiles off their faces. The floor along the passage was polished oak, carpeted in the middle. The horse gave a performance that would be the envy of an accomplished skater, smashing quite a few passage windows by way of demonstrating his versatility. He was also quite adamant that he had no intention of going down the stairs and kicked out behind him to emphasise his point, thus rapidly clearing the ring of people from around his rear quarters. The only way to persuade him to go down against his better judgement was to blindfold him and in this way he regained the garden.

During the Stewards Dinner in 1851, when some fifty people were present, Mr Fowler must have ground his teeth once again when the conversation turned to the exploit of the Marquis of Waterford, his friends and their extrovert horse, and some bright young spark was seized with the desire to outdo the Marquis and boasted that his little grey could do anything the other horse had done and more. Despite protestations from the landlord, two or three of the young blades left the room. A short time later, a rumbling sound was heard coming from the general direction of the stairs, growing nearer, until the door burst open to admit the gallant grey. The young men led him around the room and over to where a huge fire was burning in the grate. It was then that a young show-off named Manning boasted that he could jump the horse over the dining table. There were gasps of consternation from the diners who were in the middle of the third course, and a groan from Mr Fowler.

Nothing daunted, the young man leapt upon the barebacked horse and rode him into a corner of the room then, urging the horse with his heels and a slap, he cleared the table. Encouraged now by cheers from the assembly, he successfully jumped it back. One of his companions then demanded a go and rode full pelt at the table, but as he took the jump the heel of the horse caught the table cloth, sending plates, glasses and candelabra in glorious crashing confusion. By now Mr Fowler had had enough and called a halt to the whole proceedings.

This feat was talked about in inns and taverns for many years to come. The famous little grey was purchased by a renowned judge of horseflesh at great price who enjoyed pointing out that this was the horse that had jumped the dining table at the old *White Hart*.

Stand
and
Deliver!

THE route of the Oxford–London stagecoach crossed Gerrards Cross Common some two centuries ago. Hidden in
a thicket was a rider on a horse, his long black cape covering
his feet and his hat pulled down hard on his head. As the
distant rumble and rattle of the approaching London–Oxford
coach became louder there was a sudden flurry of hooves and
a clear firm voice rang out on the highway, 'Stand and
Deliver!' The coach shuddered to a halt, and the passengers
were systematically and charmingly robbed.

This gentleman of the road could have been Jack Shrimpton, who was the favourite highwayman in the area. His was
the story of 'local boy makes good'. Born in the village of
Penn, he was the son of a respectable churchwarden, who
must have found life very embarrassing because of the exploits
of his wayward son. Nevertheless, it would seem that the
people of Penn were quite proud of Jack. He was a likeable
rogue and it was said he had more brains and courage than
most in his profession. He had been just like any other child
growing up in the village, perhaps 'scrumping' the odd
orchard, but what boy worth his salt did not? At the age of
sixteen, his father sent Jack to London as an apprentice to a
soap boiler. This could not have been the most absorbing of

15

jobs, but Jack stuck it out until he had finished his apprentice-
ship. Then he went in the Army. But he hated the life and
simply could not mould himself to the discipline – so he left to
become a 'gentleman of the road'.

Knowing the countryside in that part of Buckinghamshire
so well, it naturally transpired that his sphere of operations
was mainly in the vicinity of his boyhood and the London–
Oxford road. So assiduous was he on this highway that it was
said that 'scarce a coach or a horseman could pass without
being robbed'. He took the then excessive sum of 50 guineas
from a barrister at Stokenchurch, but broke all records by
raking in his biggest haul when he held up four coaches on the
same occasion, again at Gerrards Cross, and took from the
passengers the sum of £150. It is said the landlord of the *Bull*
provided him and his horse with secret accommodation.

Calling into one of his favourite taverns in London, Jack sat
down at a table with a pleasant enough fellow and shared a
bottle of wine with him. He was amused to find, after some
time had passed in this jovial company, that he was drinking
with the public hangman. Undismayed, Jack asked a question
that had long perplexed him.

'What', he asked, 'was the reason, when you perform your
office, that you put the knot just under the left ear, for, in my
opinion, were you to fix it to the nape of the neck, it would be
more easy for the fellow being hanged?'. The hangman replied
that he had hanged a good many in his time and had not had
one complaint yet. He went on to say that should Jack ever
stand in need of this service from him, he would be delighted
to perform him that small extra favour. Jack replied that, if it
were all the same to him, he would rather do without his
favours, as from what he had heard, they generally proved
slightly dangerous!

There is no doubt that Jack was looked upon as a kind of
Robin Hood who robbed the rich to help the poor. Once he
met a couple of bailiffs near High Wycombe carrying a poor
farmer off to gaol for a debt of £6. Jack dug in his pockets and
happily paid over the debt for the farmer and obtained his

release. Afterwards he waylaid the bailiffs and recovered his money.

It must have seemed to him ironical that, after successfully evading the law for so long, he should be caught for the minor offence of living it up in Bristol, of all places, and becoming drunk and disorderly. In those times, a nightly watch was kept in most towns by a number of constables or watchmen, to keep a check on any strangers or suspicious characters. Their duties were to apprehend all those who could not give a satisfactory account of their movements. Jack was caught by one of these, who grabbed him by the scruff of the neck and was taking him in for unruly behaviour. Jack did not like this one bit. No one laid hands on the great Jack Shrimpton and got away with it. Whether intentionally or not, he killed the watchman. He was brought to trial, convicted not only of murder but also of five highway robberies, and sentenced to death. Several great men interceded on his behalf to obtain the Queen's pardon, to no avail. Jack was hanged at St Michael's Hill, Bristol on 4th September 1713 without showing the slightest sign of repentance.

With the increased spate of Enclosure Acts at the end of the 18th and the beginning of the 19th centuries, many heaths and commons were enclosed and the highwaymen lost a great deal of their cover and with it their livelihood. The era of that 'romantic' figure finally drew to a close when the railways brought an end to the days of stagecoach travel.

With the advent of the railways, Buckinghamshire experienced no 'Jesse James' train robbers. Not, that is, until our own times, when, on the night of 8th August 1963, the Glasgow–London mail train was held up and robbed at Cheddington. The Great Train Robbers got away with two and a half million pounds. What would Jack Shrimpton have thought of that?

Amersham's Brass Band

AMERSHAM'S first Brass Band sprang from the fertile mind of George Ward (1860–1943), the well-known local photographer, and was formed under the sponsorship of an organisation known as the Sons of Temperance (Amersham Division) on 27th October, 1890 at an historic meeting at the Gas Works, where George was the first manager.

Item one on the Agenda was the reading of a communication from the Bandmaster of High Wycombe Temperance Band laying down in no uncertain terms the rules to be firmly adhered to, not the least being that of complete and utter abstinence from drink at all times and in all circumstances. This having been clearly understood by all present, the Chairman was appointed with impressive ceremony and George Ward (without doubt the most versatile of the company) was appointed not only Secretary and Treasurer but also Bandmaster, in which capacity he undertook to teach every instrument in the band.

At that time, temperance meetings were held in the Market Hall with great regularity and, needless to say, sobriety, under the direction of Mrs J. Walker, a lady of impeccable repute and awesome respectability. She viewed with unmitigated and scathing scorn all those who strayed from the temperance path and kept a very wary eye on the newly formed Amersham Sons of Temperance Brass Band who were expected to be the first in attendance at her meetings, even on practice nights.

By courtesy of George Ward, the band practised in a room at the Gas Works at the price of 9d per night, including lighting and heating. Members of the Band were required to purchase their own instruments, but the matter of purchasing sheet music was not so easily overcome so George advanced the money for the first supply. The first pieces successfully mastered by the band were *Awake O Happy Nation, Old Hundredth* and *Meet me at the Fountain* (water of course). New members joined at a steady pace including such people as Will Tarbuck, the gravedigger, who suddenly found himself consumed with an overwhelming desire to master the intricacies of the valve trombone.

The Band now began to feel confident, especially when their services were sought for various engagements. On Saturday 20th June 1891, they were in the High Wycombe Parade and, in August of that year, they commenced the first of many years unforgettable attendance at the Amersham Flower Show, playing for the customary dancing in the evening. The outing of the Lower Baptist Sunday School became a regular feature too and it was unanimously agreed that the Band should parade the length of the town every Saturday evening.

A Primrose League demonstration held in Shardeloes Park on 10th September, 1891 accepted their tender, as did the Liberal Meeting at Winchmore Hill on the 23rd of that month for the fee of 15 shillings. Flourishing now, they submitted a tender to play at the Chesham Temperance Fete, playing throughout for the sum of three guineas, plus tea.

This engagement was, to a large extent, their undoing, as the first two broken pledges of temperance occurred at this event, when two members were reported to the committee for this most serious offence. With the eyes of the world and Mrs Walker upon them, the band called an emergency meeting and breathed an audible sigh of relief when it was found the charge could not be proved 'and, therefore, fell to the ground' – only to gasp again in horror as the two members concerned, stricken now to a state of unbearable contrition, voluntarily stated that they had on another occasion, solely in an effort to moisten their lips and consequently improve their musical virtuosity, broken the pledge.

The meeting held its breath – the minutes go on: 'As this information was given of their own free will and would not otherwise have been preferred against them, they were asked in good faith to re-sign the pledge, which they did, to the satisfaction of their fellows' and the restoration to comparative consciousness of Mrs Walker, with the aid of smelling salts!

The crisis over, the Band made arrangements for Christmas 1891. In the snow, clustered around the gaslight in the market square, they made the most of the pool of light, creating the right atmosphere for the season and resembling a picture on a Christmas card.

Everything seemed to be going swimmingly until the same two members were reported once again for breaking the pledge. This continued to happen with regularity and to spread among the other band members like a contagious disease so that Mrs Walker began seriously to look on the Band as an ally of the demon drink.

At a momentous meeting held on 14th March 1892, in an atmosphere charged with portent, the Band 'seriously considered severing its connection with the Sons of Temperance'. A horrified letter from the Leader of the Chesham Division Sons of Temperance was read to the meeting, in which he earnestly (in their own interests) entreated and implored the Band to reconsider the extreme seriousness of the step they were contemplating. Nevertheless, the members, after much debate and deliberation, unanimously resolved that the wisest course 'was to entirely sever all connection with the Sons of Temperance' because, in the actual wording of the minute, 'it dont appear possible for a Temperance Band to be successfully worked in Amersham'. And it was agreed also that the Band should 'henceforth be called and known as The Amersham Town Band'. Mrs Walker was not only shaken to the core, but it was said, from thenceforth was never quite the same. The Band, however, equipped now with a new sense of freedom, and smart uniforms, went on from one triumph to another.

During the First World War, the Band lapsed as members volunteered one after another to defend King and Country. Amersham was bandless until 1929, when a certain gentleman, friend of George Ward and named Herbie Fountain, manfully took up the baton and decided the time was now ripe for a town band revival. Gathering together a group of lads in their late teens or early twenties, it was not long before the Amersham Town Band was back in full swing.

Was there anything more splendid than to hear that first throb of the big bass drum, the first blare of the cornets as they swung down the wide High Street in their blue and red uniforms, stepping out in fine military style, stirring the hearts of the townsfolk and heralding some long anticipated event, whilst children either marched at their side or bobbed and danced among their ranks.

Once more the voracious appetite of war claimed so many members that it was impossible for the Band to continue. However, in 1977, it was restarted again and flourishes now more than ever, playing at competitions and fetes throughout the county. If you should see them, take a closer look and remember their story.

Murder
at
Haddenham

IF ever a man contributed to his own murder, out of sheer
stupidity, it was Noble Edden. Edden was a fine, strong,
handsome man (which was why his fellows called him 'Noble'),
who worked some land in Crendon fields where he had
established a small nursery and took his produce into Aylesbury every market day. His land lay on high ground with a
fine view of the surrounding countryside for miles around.
One day a movement caught his eye – two men were moving
across a field towards a flock of sheep. Noble saw them move
in among them and then quite distinctly he saw them kill a
sheep. What is more he recognised both men. He was glad
they could not see him, although he had a clear view of them.

It was not long before the theft was discovered and there
was quite a buzz around the countryside, but Noble Edden
kept quiet and said nothing. The year was 1828 and Noble
knew the penalty for sheep-stealing was death or transportation. He was torn, should he report what he had seen or not?
He did not want the death of two men on his conscience, and
yet he felt that justice ought to be done in some way or
another.

Every time he met the men, he just looked knowingly at
them and said meaningfully 'Baa! Baa! Baa!' If he met them in

23

the village or on the road 'Baa! Baa! Baa!', or if they were drinking with the other men in a public house, he would do the same – 'Baa! Baa! Baa!'. The two men appeared to take no notice of him, but they could hardly miss the fact that Noble knew what they had been up to and that one word from him could mean disaster for them.

One Saturday night in the October of that year, Noble had been to Aylesbury Market as usual and did not start for home until after dark. He came upon a man walking to Haddenham and he picked him up. The man recounted afterwards how Noble had told him of a strange premonition he had that something was going to happen to him. Just what, he had no idea, but the feeling was so strong that he felt compelled to tell his passenger. It was plain to the man that Noble was truly alarmed and he offered to ride all the way to Thame with him. The offer seemed to shake Noble out of his depression and he hastily declined it, saying he would be all right, and he went on alone.

Meanwhile, back in the kitchen of their cottage in Thame, Mrs Edden was happily ironing when, without the slightest warning, she was smitten with a vision. She saw quite plainly before her the figure of her husband and a man strike him over the head with a stone hammer, an extremely heavy implement used to break up stones on the highway. She recognised the man as someone known both to herself and her husband as Tyler. She cried out, albeit to herself, 'Oh, dear God, my husband is being murdered', and ran into the road crying and shouting. Doors and windows opened and the neighbours came running. They tried to tell her she had imagined it all and tried to pacify her, but still she insisted it was so. Some of the men equipped with lanterns set out on the route they knew Noble would be sure to come by, Mrs Edden with them. They walked and walked until Mrs Edden fell exhausted to the ground, but they found no trace of Noble Edden.

Anxey meadows were close to the village of Haddenam and, in those pre-enclosure days, were common grazing land. Early next morning, a farmer's man was on his way there with some horses when he came across the body of Noble. It was not a pretty sight, his head had been crushed. The man ran back to Haddenham and raised the village.

They took the body to the Cider House to await the Inquest and searched the area. They found his horse and cart about a mile away, but nowhere could they find a stranger who might have been the murderer. It looked as if whoever had killed Noble Edden had got clean away.

At the inquest the following week, a verdict was returned of 'murder by persons unknown', and the body was taken home to Mrs Edden. It was thought in those days that, if a murderer touched the body if his victim, there was sure to be a sign from that body, such as blood flowing from the ears or mouth, or perhaps the face would change colour. Hence the saying 'Murder will out!'. The moment the body was over her threshold, Mrs Edden sent for Tyler, the man she had seen strike her husband in the vision, to come and touch it. Not surprisingly, Tyler refused the invitation. She sent for him several times, but each time he refused.

Weeks passed and then months, and people were heavily suspicious of Tyler and a friend of his called Sewell. There was no real evidence against them, other than the vision of Mrs Edden and the fact that they had both been seen washing their hands in a pond on the night of the murder.

During this time, Noble Edden's son took over his father's business and visited Aylesbury Market regularly, as his father had before him. It was on just such a dark night as the one on which his father had been murdered that he was coming along the same route when two men leapt out of a high hedge and tried to jump on his cart. Young Edden was a dab hand with a whip and he beat them off. It was too dark to see their faces, but one of them called out 'We will serve you the same as we did your ole father fore long.' The other one shouted agreement. Noble's son was sure he recognised the voices of Tyler and Sewell.

And so suspicion grew against the two men, until on 16th August 1829, Sewell was arrested and charged with the murder of Noble Edden, on what evidence is not known. Sewell made a statement implicating Tyler, and was immediately committed to Aylesbury Gaol. Tyler was arrested on 19th August at Uxbridge, purely on the statement of Sewell. Both men were brought before the magistrates. Mrs Edden, the widow, was in court to tell the lengthy story of the vision and by this time she added that she had also heard the sound of her husband's voice. She swore that without the slightest doubt the man she saw commit the murder was Tyler. This, she went on to say, was proved by the fact that he refused to touch her husband's body. Sewell's statement was then read in which he stated that he had actually seen Tyler strike Edden with the hammer. For some reason, the magistrates did not believe him and told him so.

On 31st August, the two men were again before the court and this time, Sewell's mother was examined. She said that she could honestly say she was the mother of Sewell, even though she had 24 other children. Yes, she did find it confusing at times, but she could always tell one of her own. She was inclined to dismiss the whole affair on account of her son being an imbecile. This she could state with absolute certainty as, she said, it ran in the family. This statement was not in the least doubted by the court, but it did not help them resolve matters. Meanwhile, Tyler was repeating over and over again his entire innocence of the charge. The magistrates declared in a bemused state that Sewell's evidence was entirely unworthy of credit and Tyler was at once discharged. Sewell was committed for re-examination. Tyler lost no time on reaching Thame to dress gaily in ribbons whereupon he danced at the doors of all those who had given evidence against him.

Sewell was brought up again a week later, and discharged. The magistrates sternly told him that they thought he had told a 'string of falsehoods'. The moment he was outside the court, he was arrested for the theft of a pair of shoes and packed off to Oxford Gaol. However, by December of that year, he was back in Aylesbury Gaol on a charge of fowl-stealing.

Meanwhile, a sinister turn of events had taken place in Thame. Bills or papers were posted in the town threatening

Seymour, the Constable, that if he persisted in his endeavours to track down the murderers of Noble Edden, he would come to some harm. Who was behind this? Sewell was in gaol and Tyler discharged.

Sewell was sentenced to fourteen years transportation for stealing the chicken and, in an attempt to commute his sentence, he said he would at last speak the truth about the murder of poor Noble Edden. This time, for some inexplicable reason, he was believed when he said Tyler 'had done the deed'. Tyler was once again arrested and the two men brought to trial.

On Friday, 5th March 1830, crowds rushed to County Hall, Aylesbury, to the trial of Tyler and Sewell. The trial took the whole of the day, during which Sewell appeared 'silly', perhaps to give credence to the evidence of his mother, and repeatedly waved to an acquaintance in the gallery. The two men declared they were as 'innocent as babes', but they were sentenced to be hanged on the following Monday, their bodies later to be dissected at the London Hospitals.

In those days, the law required that those convicted of murder be sentenced immediately after trial, and executed within 48 hours, but those tried on a Friday had a day longer to live, as it was not considered proper to hang a man on the Sabbath. Therefore, on Monday 8th March, it was estimated that some five thousand people assembled outside Aylesbury gaol to witness the execution of Tyler and Sewell. Sewell was first to appear on the scaffold and he kept up the idiotic conduct as before. He looked searchingly among the crowds as if anxiously expecting someone he knew to be there. At last he saw him and shouted out 'Ah! There you are. I'm just about to die and I hope I shall go to heaven; so goodbye, Mr Taylor, goodbye.' Tyler was nervous and trembling but he stepped forward and in a firm voice declared his innocence to the crowd and said he met his fate due to false swearers. He was about to say something else, but the cap was drawn over both their faces and the next moment all was ended.

Or was it? Did those two men really kill Noble Edden. Or was there someone in that crowd who knew differently?

The Olney Pancake Race

THE Olney Pancake Race, held naturally enough on Shrove Tuesday, has been going on since the year 1455 when pancakes were as popular as pizzas are today. Exactly how it originated is not definitely known, but there is the story that some medieval housewife was caught in mid-pancake when the Shriving bell clanged calling her to church and she, anxious to embark upon Lent free from all sin, rushed to the church with pancake and frying pan still in her hand.

Be that as it may, Shrovetide has always been a good excuse for having that last fling before an austere Lent and was marked by merry-making, eating and drinking. In Olney, it was celebrated as a Festival and the custom of the race has continued down through the centuries, save for a brief lapse here and there.

Only those who have been permanent residents of the town for at least three months may qualify for the Race and are required to wear the housewives' traditional uniform, namely an apron and headcovering.

At precisely 11.30 am on the day, the first warning bell is rung, telling competitors to commence to fry pancakes. Pans start sizzling, then a quarter of an hour later, the second warning bell is heard telling them to now make their way to the Market Square together with freshly made pancake and frying pan. They must 'toss' once whilst under starter's orders – the cry goes up 'Toss pancakes – are you ready?' The Pancake Bell rings and they are off!

Helter skelter through the town they go, bearing their frying pans in one hand in front of them, which is certainly not as easy as it sounds. It is the rule that they must toss twice during the course of the race, which usually has the spectators screaming with excitement as pancakes are dropped or caught, and then toss once more on entering the churchyard, where the winner receives the most coveted prize of a kiss from the Ringer of the Pancake Bell.

At noon the Parish Church is packed for the Shriving Service. Competitors place their pans around the font before occupying seats reserved for them in the chancel. A highlight of the service is the singing of the famous Olney hymns, composed in the 18th century by two of Olney's most famous residents – William Cowper, the poet, and his friend, the Reverend John Newton, a former slave trader and curate of the Parish Church. A strange combination, but they produced some of the loveliest hymns that are now part of the English language. The day usually ends with a Pancake Party.

For years now people have come from far and wide to see the Olney Pancake Race. After the last War, far away in the United States of America, the townsfolk of Liberal, Kansas, saw press pictures of the race and decided to add it to their own Shrove Tuesday celebrations. In 1950, they took it one step further and issued a challenge to the housewives of Olney for the two towns to compete for a trophy in the form of an engraved skillet to be known as the Transatlantic Pancake Trophy. The race is now run annually in both towns on a time basis, and a transatlantic call goes from Liberal to Olney Vicarage to compare times and declare the winner.

Internationally famous, the race has been filmed and shown on television in both countries, and has done much to cement Anglo-American relations. It also manages to remain good fun at the same time!

John Hampden's Body

O N a day in July, 1828 the afternoon sun beamed through the windows of Great Hampden Church, spreading patterns on the stone floor. The small group of men stood quiet and still. They neither looked at one another nor spoke. There appeared a hang-dog look about them, almost of guilt. They had come to exhume the body of the great patriot, John Hampden, who had died as a result of wounds received at the Battle of Chalgrove Field in June 1643.

Lord Nugent, the biographer of Hampden and instigator of the present disturbance of his body, leaned eagerly forward, peering into the dark depths of the vault. He hoped to solve once and for all the mystery of Hampden's death, exactly how he had received that last mortal wound. Was it as a result of two carbine balls in the shoulder received from the enemy, or was it due to the bursting of his own pistol in his hand?

The people of the surrounding countryside had heard of this proposed exhumation and were quite scandalised. If anyone was their hero, it was John Hampden. Born into an ancient Buckinghamshire family, his grandfather, Griffith Hampden, had entertained the great Queen Elizabeth at the family home, Hampden House, which stood close by to the church. John had been educated at the Free Grammar School at Thame and then at Magdalen College at Oxford. He had married and lived a very happy family life at Hampden

House. Cousin to Oliver Cromwell, he had been MP for Wendover through five Parliaments and later represented the County in those troublesome times between King Charles I and Parliament.

In 1635, in the church at Great Kimble, only a few miles from Hampden, he and others had made their stand and refused to pay the illegally levied Ship Money. His popularity with the yeomen and farmers in the district had known no bounds. Here was one man who they could trust implicitly. So much so that when, in 1642, the King was seeking the arrest of Hampden for his part in the Grand Remonstrance (a catalogue of Charles' misdeeds) some 6,000 men from Buckinghamshire had marched to London with petitions on his behalf 'in whose loyalty we, his countrymen and neighbours, have ever had cause to confide.' He proved himself to be a man of firmness and mettle, both in the House and in the fighting that ensued.

On that fateful day in 1643, he had been with his 'Greenjackets' at Watlington when he received word that Prince Rupert's forces were planning to ambush a convoy carrying £21,000 pay for the Parliamentary Army at High Wycombe. He immediately set out with his troops to delay Rupert, who turned and stood at Chalgrove. Hampden's first charge was thrown back, but he rallied his forces and charged again. Almost immediately he was seen to sway in the saddle, his right arm hanging lifeless at his side, and to fall on his horse's neck. Desperately, he tried to make for Pyrton in Oxfordshire, the home of his first wife, but the enemy cut him off. In great agony, he headed for Thame where years before he had attended school and where he knew good friends would look after him. He died there on 24th June 1643.

It had been assumed and recorded that Hampden died as a result of the shattering of his shoulder by two carbine balls. But some years later, Sir Robert Pye, a Colonel in the Parliamentary Army who had married Hampden's daughter, told a remarkable story. He said that as John Hampden led the second charge at Chalgrove, his own pistol had burst and shattered his arm in a terrible manner. He also said that his father-in-law, as he lay dying at Thame, had sent for him and informed him, weak as he was, that he lay the blame for his inevitable death to a large extent at Sir Robert's door, as the offending pistol had been one of a brace that was a present from him. A distraught Sir Robert assured him that he had bought both pistols from one of the most reputable gunmakers in Paris and further, he had indeed fired and proved them himself. Sir Robert then hastened to examine the other pistol of the pair and found that it was loaded to the muzzle, crammed with charges. It was concluded that the servant who had been given the regular morning task of loading his master's pistols had done so very diligently, but without drawing any former charges.

All the troops that could be spared, drums muffled and arms reversed, carried the body of John Hampden through his beloved Chiltern beechwoods to his Hampden home for its final rest. How often he had walked those high, breezy hills, had stood and gazed at the long views of the countryside he so dearly loved. His countrymen mourned the loss of this gallant man, respected by friend and foe alike. Yet it appears strange that John Hampden was buried without so much as his grave being marked with a commemorative word.

And now, all those years later, on that afternoon of the 21st July 1828, the silence in Great Hampden Church was broken by the sound of coffins scraping over the stone floor beneath. Lord Nugent could stand it no longer and leapt into the vault. The name plate of the coffin which lay next to that of the wife of John Hampden was corroded beyond recognition. It obviously belonged to a person of quality and they felt that without doubt this must be the one of the 'Patriot'. The local plumber opened it, and propped the body up with a spade. After 185 years the muscles of the face had not completely disappeared. They found the shoulder bones showed no signs whatever of having been broken, but the right hand was severed from the

33

arm. This surely would give credence to the story of Sir Robert Pye, as everyone was as certain as they could be that this was the coffin of John Hampden.

However, to the complete astonishment of all, Lord Nugent, when he eventually wrote his book, glossed over the findings and gave the impression that more likely than not they had opened up the wrong coffin. Whether his attitude was brought about through pressure of public opinion is not known.

There was one present on that day in the church at Great Hampden who was convinced beyond any doubt that it was indeed the body of John Hampden that had been exhumed. He was Mr Roberts, a confidential servant at nearby Hampden House. He had looked down into the vault and seen the face of the body in the coffin and could not forget it. The very first time he ascended the stairs in Hampden House after the exhumation, he felt one of the portraits hanging high on the stairs looking down at him. He instantly recognised the face as the one in the grave in the church. He informed his employer, the Earl of Buckingham, who ordered the picture to be taken down. Together they examined it closely – they removed a piece of old canvas and there underneath was the name – JOHN HAMPDEN 1640.

The Dinton Hermit

WHEN King Charles II stepped off the boat at Dover on 25th May 1660 after many years in exile, the whole country seemed to go mad with joy. Church bells rang, people cheered and danced, and plans were made to mark the occasion in every kind of festive way. When he reached London, it was the same – cheers and celebrations all the way. But there were two men in the village of Dinton in Buckinghamshire who did not feel quite so elated and certainly did not join in any festivities.

Simon Mayne of Dinton Hall had been a Justice of the Peace and Member of Parliament for Aylesbury throughout the whole of the Protectorate. A close friend of Oliver Cromwell and a strong Parliamentarian, he had entertained Oliver at the Hall after the Battle of Naseby and Oliver, in an uncharacteristic rush of affection, had marked the occasion by presenting his host with the gift of his sword. As if all this was not enough, Mayne had also been a member of the Commission that had drawn up the warrant for the execution of King Charles I and, even worse, was one of the signatories to that document. He was brought to trial and was sentenced to imprisonment in the Tower.

All the troubles of these tempestuous times seemed seriously to upset another gentleman of Dinton. John Bigg, a former medical student of great learning and clerk to Simon Mayne,

suddenly went into a chronic state of melancholy and betook himself to a nearby underground cave where he hid himself away. From there he rarely strayed, save for the summer months when, perhaps as some kind of holiday, he was known to frequent the woods near Kimble. He lived the life of a recluse for many years, relying entirely on the kindness of the people of Dinton for his food and drink, though he did not beg for it – he begged only for leather and cloth to patch and repair his clothes and shoes, which he never changed. Consequently his clothes became a mosaic of patchwork and, when he succeeded in obtaining a piece of leather, he patched it immediately to his boots, until it was said 'they became more than tenfold thickness'. One of these shoes is in the Ashmolean Museum at Oxford. It is vastly large and thought to consist of approximately one thousand pieces of leather.

A portrait from a drawing of John Bigg published in 1787 appears in Lipscombe's History of the County of Buckinghamshire and 'represents a man of not ill features, an open countenance devoid of moroseness, severity and vulgarity'. He wore a two-peaked hood of apparently the same patched materials, a short cloak and a girdle or belt from which hung three bottles, one for strong beer, one for small beer and one for milk. He leaned on a three-pronged fork and his trousers or pantaloons did not quite meet his shoes. A strange figure and a frightening one to those who did not know him. Sir Thomas Lee of Hartwell said that, as a boy, he had lived in terror of meeting the Dinton Hermit.

Bigg appears to have lived quite adequately with just the bare material needs he received from the kind people of Dinton. If we are to take notice of the description of his face, he seems to have recovered from his first fit of melancholy and passed into a state of comparative content. At any rate, he remained a hermit until he died and was buried in Dinton in 1696.

It has often been said that this weird character, consumed with remorse, had hidden himself away in 1660 because he was in fact one of the pair of grim, black-hooded executioners who had brought the life of Kings Charles I to an end so abruptly with an axe on the scaffold in Whitehall in 1649. Despite attempts immediately after the Restoration to discover the identity of those two gentlemen, it was never revealed who they were or which one had actually struck the fatal blow. The Commissioners questioned many eyewitnesses, who put forward a variety of names. Some were under the impression that it had been the common Hangman. But without exception all stated that the man was young, no older than 20. And John Bigg had been born in 1629!

The
Chiltern Hundreds

WHAT are the Chiltern Hundreds and how did they come about? This is a common question asked by newcomers to Buckinghamshire.

The origin of the Hundreds is obscure, but a Hundred appears to have been a Saxon institution, perhaps the grouping together of a hundred hides of land or even a hundred families. But certainly a Hundred is a sub-division of a Shire with its own Court.

The Shire Court met twice yearly – the Hundred Court met once a month and so could bring a swifter justice to the wrongdoers of the area. In the Chilterns there are three such Hundreds – Burnham, Stoke and Desborough: the Chiltern Hundreds.

Matthew Paris, of the cloister of St Albans, was something more than just a chronicler. He was an acute observer and an excellent historian. He wrote in the 13th century that the hills known as the Chilterns were of such a wild nature, thickly forested so as to provide good cover, with upland commons and wild heaths, that they were the common haunt of large marauding bands of outlaws, not to mention wild beasts. A traveller took his life in his hands when he travelled through this part of the country and could expect to be molested, robbed or even murdered.

Matthew Paris goes on to say that, as far back as the 10th century, Leofstan, the twelfth Abbot of St Albans, ordered some of the woods to be chopped down, hoping that this would improve matters. He also granted some lands to a fellow called Thurnoth on condition that he would protect the people of the district from the plundering robbers. Yet the frightening state of lawlessness in the hills persisted, giving rise to the old Chiltern saying 'Here if you beat a bush, it's odds you'll start a thief.'

In the absence of anything remotely resembling an organised police force, swift justice was necessary to get rid of the malefactors efficiently, and Stewards of the Chiltern Hundreds were appointed to bring some kind of order to the area, with the help of their retainers. This Stewardship was a Crown appointment and paid but little. A felon was usually hanged in sight of the woods so that his fellows could see and take example. Place names today give clues as to where these long-lost gibbets stood stark against the skyline – Gallows Hill, Hangings Hill, Hang Alley etc.

The Hundred Courts met in the open, unless the weather turned for the worse when they quickly made for the nearest town. The Court sat in a ring or square of four benches, hence 'within the four benches of the Hundred.' They dealt with criminal and minor ecclesiastical matters and also levied taxes. In the Danelaw Counties, these Courts were called Wapentakes. Traces of these Hundred Courts and Wapentakes can still be found in different parts of the country. At High Wycombe there is such an earthwork in the shape of a ring – Desborough Castle – and it is thought to be the site of the old Desborough Hundred Court.

As manorial and parochial administration gradually came to the fore, the influence of the old Hundred Courts waned. Nevertheless, the position of Steward of the Chiltern Hundreds, an office of honour with negligible profit, remained. Therefore, if a Member of Parliament wished to give up his seat during mid-term, he could not throw off his duty to his constituents so easily – but, if he accepted an office under the Crown, however small the profit, his seat automatically became vacant. And so, over the years, this method has been used by those Members wishing to resign – they apply for the Chiltern Hundreds!

Railway
Fever

THERE was no doubt about it – the coming of the Railway to Buckinghamshire at the beginning of the last century was not welcomed. The 'monster navigated by a tail of smoke and sulphur', was certainly not looked upon with equanimity by the people of a quiet, rural county. It was thought that to allow this huffing, puffing, horseless carriage to rampage across the countryside would only bring trouble in its wake, separating communities and ruining towns and villages. It was even thought that it would cause pregnant cows to abort in sheer terror.

It was hardly surprising, therefore, that when the first plan was put forward in 1825 by George Stephenson for a railway line from London to Birmingham, it caused more than a little uproar. The county of Buckinghamshire lay directly in the path of the route which was to run by way of Uxbridge, through the Misbourne Valley to the Wendover Gap in the Chiltern Hills, then on to Aylesbury, Coventry and Birmingham. But every landowner, from Hillingdon right the way through to Wendover, objected, including the Duke of Buckingham and any that came under his influence. These large landowners were powerful and their objections not to be taken lightly and they were joined by protests from wagon and coach proprietors, not to mention turnpike trustees. Stephenson, in the light of such opposition was compelled to seek another route and instead had to go for the Tring Gap in the Chilterns as opposed to the one at Wendover.

This meant a new route which ran further to the east via Watford, Tring and Bletchley. Here again he met with opposition from landowners and others, and he was forced over to the other side of Watford, which necessitated a spending of at least another quarter of a million pounds. The new route obtained Parliamentary approval on 6th May 1833 and, approximately one year later, construction of the line started.

The closest the final route passed to the town of Aylesbury was at Cheddington, some ten miles away, and this did not please the townspeople one bit. In their opinion, the line by-passed the most important town in Buckinghamshire, and surely they, more than any, needed an easy route through to London. Some of Aylesbury's most prominent citizens decided to hold a meeting at the *White Hart Inn* in November 1835 to investigate the possibility of forming their own Railway Company, which could run a branch line from Aylesbury to Cheddington.

Among the indignant gathering were George Carrington from Missenden Abbey and Sir Harry Verney of Claydon House. From this meeting was born the Aylesbury Railway Company, the Aylesbury Railway Act receiving Royal Assent in May of the following year. Stephenson's son, Robert, was appointed Engineer and construction actually started in December 1837, finishing over a year later. The little Aylesbury Railway to Cheddington was the fiirst branch line which directly connected with the London–Birmingham line.

The official opening took place on 15th June 1839 and the day was proclaimed a public holiday. From six o'clock in the morning, bands paraded the streets and a general air of excitement pervaded the town. People from the surrounding areas flooded in, passengers swamped the terminus, and the first train out to Cheddington was packed. Just to add a touch of class, a special train carrying the important and dignified Directors of the London–Birmingham Railway left Euston at noon and headed for Aylesbury to join in the celebrations. A banquet was held at the *White Hart* where the health of Robert Stephenson was proposed. He replied most genially that whatever might occur in the future, his audience could rely upon it that the London and Birmingham Railway would never forget its eldest child, the Aylesbury Railway. The assembly was much moved! But how they roared with laughter when Dr Lee of Hartwell House, in his speech, prophesied that the day would come when there would be more railways, for example to Thame (more laughter), Princes Risborough and Wendover (absolute convulsions).

The Cheddington Line was a success. Many people availed themselves of the service, providing a continuous stream of passengers. The journey to Cheddington took about ten minutes and it then took another couple of hours to London. The local coach services taking four hours to reach London were unable to compete. In only seven years, because it was so successful, and in order to forestall any outsiders, the mighty London and Birmingham purchased the local Aylesbury Company and it merged with the main line system.

By this time, railway fever had many in its grip, even some of those that had opposed it in the first place. Sir Harry Verney and the Duke of Buckingham set up and built the Buckinghamshire Railway. The section from Bletchley to Banbury was opened in 1850 and the section from Claydon (Verney Junction) to Oxford, the following year.

It was some time after this that some representatives of the Great Northern Railway arrived at the *White Hart Inn* to consult the proprietor, Mr J. K. Fowler, about the prospects of building a line from Aylesbury to Thame. 'J.K.' advised them against this. He suggested instead a route from Aylesbury, passing through Quainton, to Claydon where it could join the latest Buckinghamshire Railway. In order to illustrate, he took the gentlemen on a trip over his proposed route, calling on the Duke of Buckingham at Wotton, near Quainton. His Grace was very keen on the idea. The party then went on to Claydon where Sir Harry Verney became very excited and asked to be counted in on the scheme. The third Duke of Buckingham became the Chairman of the new company, Sir

Harry Verney the Deputy Chairman and J. K. Fowler one of the Directors. The line was opened in 1868. The Duke quietly used his influence so that the line ran closer to his estates at Wotton than originally planned and at Claydon, where the two railways met, a new station was constructed, named Verney Junction.

After all the work on that project was completed, the Duke felt the time had come to construct a private horsedrawn tramway (so called because it was to run alongside the road). The new track was to be a branch off the Aylesbury–Buckingham from Quainton to Wotton and His Grace envisaged all kinds of agricultural produce and passengers travelling with comparative ease into Aylesbury, with such commodities as coal travelling back. He was also of the opinion that, as the route was to run over private property, the greater part owned by himself, Parliamentary approval would not be necessary, and so he resolutely went ahead regardless of the public highways he crossed in so doing. Luckily, it did turn out that the tramway was covered under an Act that allowed construction to commence, subject to certain restrictions with regard to weight and speed, which the Wotton Tramway did not appear to violate.

Work started on the line in September 1870 and the Duke employed his estate workers for the labouring. This suited them very well, as it provided work in winter, which was always a slack season for all working on the land.

The rail was duly laid to run from Quainton Road Station, through Waddesdon and via Westcott village to Wotton and His Grace managed to navigate the track to go so close to his Manor that it ran under the very windows of the Thame Lodge House. On 1st April 1871, the official opening of the line from Quainton to Wotton took place in the shape of a ceremony attended by the Duke.

The people of the village of Brill, a half a mile away, looked on with envy. By the end of the year they had asked the Duke if the line could possibly be extended as far as the bottom of Brill Hill. The Duke had already thought of this and was only too pleased to comply in order to provide a passenger service.

The station at Brill was opened in 1872, and passengers from Brill thenceforth appreciated the fact that in winter the boy at Wotton Station was ordered to keep a kettle boiling so as to provide hot water bottles for frozen travellers.

The little tramway flourished to such an extent that, with the increasing passengers and cargo, the horses which pulled them could no longer cope and the Duke was asked by his manager if he would contemplate the purchase of two engines. By 1872, steam locomotives had taken over from the horses.

The change over to mechanical means took some getting used to by those who had always dealt with horses and there were one or two mishaps. In November 1872, the flywheel broke off No 2 Engine and went careering back down the line. The eighteen passengers were forced to walk into the village of Westcott and a Mr Cook, who had always averred he had no time for these new-fangled transport arrangements, took them into Quainton in his milk cart feeling very superior.

In 1892, the Metropolitan line reached Aylesbury. It had come down in faltering stages by the direct route first envisaged by George Stephenson for the London–Birmingham railway, first stopping at Rickmansworth and later on, emerging through the Wendover Gap.

The closing day of the Wotton Tramway took place on 30th November 1935 when the last train pulled out of Brill station packed with people singing *Auld Lang Syne*. Cars and cycles then raced to Quainton Road where the rails were severed at the stroke of midnight.

The upheaval caused by the coming of the railway in the last century has long since blended into the landscape and it is strange to think that the invasion so bitterly resisted should now be looked back on with nostalgia. At Quainton Road today, the headquarters of the Quainton Railway Society, the old atmosphere is wonderfully re-created by the engines and coaches of the past that are on display. Somehow there is nothing so sad as the sight of a disused railway line with tall grass sprouting from between the sleepers, a permanently fallen signal or an empty station full of ghosts.

44

Primroses and Disraeli

THE most distinguished person to live in Buckinghamshire in the last century was without doubt the Prime Minister of England, Benjamin Disraeli. The local people were filled with pride to count such a man as one of them – yet it had not always been so. There was a time when the young Disraeli was given a rough passage from some of the landed gentry and the electors of the county.

He was born in London in 1804, the son of Isaac D'Israeli, a man with an insatiable love of books and the author of the renowned *Curiosities of Literature*. It was not surprising therefore that Benjamin grew up in the most profound literary atmosphere. In the summer months they rented Hyde House at Hyde Heath, a small hamlet between Chesham and Amersham and it was here that Benjamin began his novel, *Vivian Grey*.

However, Isaac began to worry about the 'precarious health' of some of his family and the 'hourly seductions' to be found in London. They had all grown to love the Chilterns and so looked for permanent residence there, eventually settling at the Manor House at Bradenham. It was a large, airy house and suited the family down to the ground.

In the June of 1832, young Benjamin decided to stand as an

Independent candidate in a By-Election at the nearby town of Wycombe against no less an opponent than Colonel Grey, the son of the then Prime Minister, Earl Grey. He chose for his colours pink and white and boldly drove into High Wycombe in an open carriage and four. Disraeli was an outlandish dresser at the best of times and, on this important day, he really excelled himself. His hair hung in long black curls, and he wore a laced shirt with a flowered waistcoat and pink lining. Quite dazzling to the drab electors of the town! He listened with contempt to the first speech made by his rival, Colonel Grey. And then it was Disraeli's turn. He wrote afterwards that 'I jumped upon the portico of the Red Lion and gave it to them for an hour and a quarter—I can give you no idea of the effect. I made them all mad—a great many of them absolutely cried. . . . All the women were on my side and wear my colours. . . .' On top of the portico stood a rather impressive life-sized model of a red lion. Carried away with the power of his own oratory, Disraeli pointed to the head of the lion and said 'When the Poll is declared, I shall be there' and then, pointing to its tail, 'and my opponent will be there.' He was quite wrong. The positions were reversed. No more than 32 votes were cast, only 12 of them for Disraeli.

Scheduled for greatness, Disraeli was not deterred. In December of the same year, he stood again at Wycombe in the General Election. He was absolutely convinced that this time he would succeed, and even went so far, in this town of chairmakers, to order a special chair to be made in his pink and white colours, for the sole purpose of carrying him around the town in splendour and triumph after his win. Once again he was wrong and he lost.

In all he tried three times to be returned at Wycombe to no avail and at last he was forced to the decision that, if he was to realise his ambition, he must of necessity join one of the political parties. The question was which? He had least time for the Whigs, so he joined the Tories. He was selected by them to stand for Taunton in Somerset. Here he polished his unique talent for oratory, but again he lost.

In 1837, his friend Wyndham Lewis was successfully

returned as the Tory Member for Maidstone, but unfortunately, several weeks later, he died, leaving his wife a rich widow and creating a By-Election. Disraeli stood in his friend's vacated shoes for the Tories and – won! A fortnight later, he rose in the House, full of confidence, to make his maiden speech. It was a disaster. He was far too self assured for a new boy and found himself at the receiving end of a resounding barracking of cat-calls, groans and even animal noises. Eventually, he was forced to sit down, but not before he had made himself heard above the din with the prophetic remark, 'Though I sit down now, the time will come when you will hear me.'

Disraeli had never really cared about money. He had often been in debt, but somehow or other there was always someone to help him out, his father or friends. But now he knew that to further his ambitions, money was necessary. He had always said that he would never be fool enough to marry for love, adding that those of his friends who had done so 'either beat their wives or lived apart from them'. He knew one rich widow, Mary Anne Wyndham Lewis, and, after a decent length of time, he began to write to her. At first she had irritated him beyond belief – she was extremely talkative. Some thought her stupid, but she was far from that. She told him in their early friendship that she liked the strong, silent type of man, and having listened to her incessant chatter for some hours, he replied that he was not surprised.

She called him 'Dizzy' and, surprisingly, the more he pursued her, the more they both began to be caught up in something for which they had not quite bargained. They were married at St George's, Hanover Square and left for a two month honeymoon. To the astonishment of all their friends, they were perfectly happy and remained so for the rest of their lives together. She adored him and he was utterly devoted to her. In later years, Mary Anne was to say to a friend: 'Dizzy married me for my money, but if he had the chance again, he would marry me for love.'

In 1847, remembering those early days of rebuff at

Wycombe, it was with a great feeling of satisfaction that he was elected the Member for Buckinghamshire and, shortly afterwards, he and Mary Anne purchased Hughenden Manor. He must have known the surroundings well as it was so close to the Bradenham of his youth. The price of the property was £35,000 and they could only lay down £15,000. He once again received help from his dear old father, friends and a mortgage from his bank.

The Disraeli's adored Hughenden. There were the usual magnificent Buckinghamshire beeches and on the slopes in the spring there were thickly sprinkled his favourite flowers, primroses. The stream below broadened into a lake and was the home of two pure white swans, Hero and Leander. From the lawns there was a distant view of Wycombe with the blue hills in the far distance. Every moment they could, the couple slipped away from London to their home, 'I want to get back to my woods and watch the burst of spring.'

He wrote that 'the chief business of Mrs Disraeli is to adorn the terrace in the Italian style', and when it was finished, 'We have restored the house to what it was before the Civil War and we have made a garden of terraces in which Cavaliers might saunter with their lady loves.' Someone told him he could not have a terrace without peacocks and, shortly afterwards, the tall, stately creatures glided up and down. Disraeli never became perhaps the true country Squire of those days because he could never really take to hunting and shooting. To him, there was nothing to compare with a ride through the woods and parkland in pony and trap with his Mary Anne at his side.

After a period in the office of Chancellor of the Exchequer, he became Prime Minister. His friendship grew with Queen Victoria, who much preferred him to Mr Gladstone, and he was invited to the wedding of the Prince of Wales. When the Queen lost her beloved Albert she found solace in the sympathetic understanding of her Minister, especially after 1872 when the death of his own Mary Anne took place. Alone, he spent more and more time at Hughenden, watching the graceful peacocks passing to and fro along the terrace they had created together.

In 1874 he went on to a second administration, but in 1876 he made his last speech in the Commons. The Queen, who cared for him and genuinely worried about his health, created him Earl of Beaconsfield. In the winter of 1877 he received a visit from her at Hughenden in the company of her daughter, Princess Beatrice. This was a very great honour for the elder statesman.

A few years later, on his last trip home to Hughenden from London, he called on his friend and solicitor, Sir Philip Rose, who owned the estate of Rayners near Wycombe. He was taken ill shortly afterwards and did not recover. As he slowly sank, a message from the Queen was whispered to him. She offered to come and see him if he so desired. With a glimmer of his old smile, he replied 'Better not—she would only ask me to take a message to Albert.'

He died in London on 19th April 1881, and by his wish his body was interred at Hughenden. Queen Victoria visited his tomb some three days after the funeral and decided to take the exact route her old friend had taken on his last trip home, via the Rayners estate. The groom was instructed to conduct her along the tracks of the great statesman to the gate leading to Hughenden. She laid a wreath of his favourite primroses on his tomb.

On the first anniversary of his death, some of his admirers started the custom of wearing primroses in their buttonholes. From this grew the Primrose League, which was organised to perpetuate Disraeli's memory and the ideas associated with him.

Disraeli once remarked to his friend, Matthew Arnold, that everyone loved flattery, and that when it came to Royalty it should be laid on with a trowel. It is perhaps revealing that Queen Victoria had inscribed on the memorial tablet above Disraeli's pew in Hughenden Church the words:

'Kings love him that speaketh right.'

Judgement Day at Water Stratford

IT is hard to credit that the small, peaceful village of Water Stratford, some two miles from Buckingham, was once the scene of disturbance and religious excitement on a scale unsurpassed at the end of the 17th century. It is also difficult to comprehend why it was that Water Stratford should have been chosen, from anywhere else on this earth, as the haven for the select few to be saved when the Day of Judgement was at hand. It was all due to the Reverend John Mason, Rector there from 1674 until his death in 1694.

He had seemed a gentle enough person and a man of moderate views when he arrived to take up his post. It had been said that at some time in his youth he may have nursed certain Calvinistic sympathies, but they didn't show. In fact, the villagers, who enjoyed tranquil lives, were quite proud of his fame as a hymn writer of some skill and he was always an exciting preacher. His wife was an unusually attractive person, both in physical appearance and personality, and the couple lived happily among the villagers for some sixteen years, during which time the Reverend revealed himself as a good and pious man.

But things can change! John Mason received three successive blows. First, the Church refused the Scripture Chronology it had taken him years to compile and he grieved over his wasted time. Secondly, his great friend, Mr Wrexham, died, and this was quickly followed by the death of his own dear wife. Almost overnight, John Mason changed and his grief was never to leave him. He began to experience strange dreams, nightmares and delusions, which he just could not shake off. They started to have an effect on his everyday life and his preaching took on a different dimension. He began to talk of a second advent and to boom on about the Day of Judgement. He would prepare his sermon for the coming Sunday well in advance, keeping it entirely free of his latest ideas, but it was no good, when he stood in the pulpit, some inner force compelled him to speak. He was convinced he was Elias, sent to herald the fact that Water Stratford had been chosen as the Holy Ground, where the good and privileged few could gather to await the day – all others outside this sphere would be destroyed by fire and sword. He endorsed all this in a pamphlet called *The Midnight Cry*, which was taken up far and wide and preached upon by others.

Naturally, his congregation at Water Stratford Church swelled, due to people coming from outside the district to hear him. So great became the crowds that he was forced to address a packed churchyard through one of the church windows – sometimes his audience was well over a thousand people, and the villagers were hard put to get into their own church.

Worse was yet to come! Hundreds of people from miles around who believed him sold their property and descended on Water Stratford in droves, filling up the houses, barns and outhouses and pitching tents on what they thought was the Holy Ground. Water Stratford became Mount Zion and here they expected to live in harmony and equality until the great day. They brought with them mountains of food supplies and livestock of all shapes and sizes, as they had no idea of how long they might have to wait. They kept up a perpetual, hideous din both day and night. Accompanied by pipes, violins and tabors, they sang hymns, dancing and clapping their hands in mass hysteria. Water Stratford was further engulfed with people coming to see the antics of these performers. Even more arrived professing to be believers just to receive free board and lodging.

It was not surprising, therefore, that the Church became alarmed and asked the Reverend Maurice, Rector of Tyringham and friend of John Mason for some twenty years, to make an impartial report. The Reverend Maurice did not relish the assignment, but set off for Water Stratford determined to do his best. On his arrival at the Rectory, he was more than a little dismayed to see people dancing about the yard, singing and chanting in loud voices. If that upset him, it was nothing to the sight that met his eyes on entering the house. It made Bedlam seem like a quiet afternoon tea party. Men, women and children were running up and down the stairs, singing and bellowing as loud as they could, laughing and clapping hands, all affecting to greet the Day of Judgement with such overwhelming elation and energy that some were quite black in the face. And when they dropped from sheer exhaustion, another group came in and took up the same procedure. And, in a garret at the top of the house, the Reverend John Mason lay dying.

He was being nursed by his devoted sister, who warned the Reverend Maurice that her brother had recently been afflicted with a severe disorder of the tongue and could not speak. Nevertheless, he was allowed to see him, but was asked only to speak of everyday, mundane matters and not to ask questions or discuss in any way her brother's rather startling recent pronouncements. If he wanted answers to questions of a religious nature, he was to ask two of the many disciples who were called 'Witnesses'. John Mason listened pleasantly enough whilst his old friend talked of ordinary matters, but the moment he touched upon recent events, he signalled for his sister to take him away.

The Reverend Maurice was taken to a downstairs room to confront the two 'Witnesses', who were courteous enough at first, but when he came to ask pointed questions and informed them he could not agree with their beliefs, they told him he would be damned and asked him to leave.

The Reverend John Mason died less than a month later, and despite the fact that he had prophesied often enough that his body would be resurrected in three days, there were those who hoped his demise would be the end of it all. But after the three days were up, the din grew no less and the crowds still hung around the Holy Ground, some saying they had seen and talked with John Mason since his death. In order to disprove this and in sheer desperation, Mason's successor, the Reverend Rushworth, opened up his predecessor's grave and displayed his corpse for all to view. Yet many still believed and stayed on the Holy Ground for up to sixteen years afterwards.

The Report of the Reverend Maurice was a fair, unbiased account. He asserted that he knew John Mason to be genuine and that he had honestly believed that Water Stratford was set apart by God.

He summed the whole thing up by saying that the delusion of John Mason was brought about by too much tobacco. He said he had seldom visited him in the past without being enveloped in clouds of smoke. This had obviously overheated Mason's brain and so kindled that zeal that brought about his end. So smoking had its drawbacks, even in those days!

All
For Love

ONE day in the year 1659, Walter Ellwood rode along the Misbourne Valley accompanied by his son, Thomas. They had ridden over the hills from their home at Crowell in Oxfordshire to visit old friends they had not seen for many years. It had been during the Civil War, whilst they were living in London, that Walter had befriended the young widow, Lady Springett and her daughter, Gulielma. The two children, Tom and Guli, had spent happy hours playing together, until Lady Springett had married Isaac Penington and moved away to live first at The Grange, Chalfont St Peter and then at Bury Farm, Amersham, where she was now known as just plain Mary Penington.

Father and son were made welcome by Isaac and Mary, who had become Quakers, but Tom wasted no time before he went to look for Guli. He recorded their meeting as follows: 'I found her gathering flowers in the garden, attended by her maid, who was also a Quaker. But when I addressed myself to her after my accustomed manner, with the intention to engage her in some discourse on the footing of our former acquaintance, though she treated me with courteous mien . . . the gravity of her look and behaviour struck such an awe upon me, that I found myself not so much master of myself. . . . Wherefore, asking pardon for my boldness in having intruded into her private walks, I withdrew not without some disorder of mind.'

After his return to Crowell, he was restless and bored until he could return to the hospitality of the Penington family. He stayed with them frequently and eventually became a Quaker himself. His father was filled with disgust at that and on one occasion told him forcibly 'Sirrah, if ever I hear you say "thou" or "thee" to me again, I'll strike your teeth down your throat.' Things went from bad to worse until Tom made up his mind that he could stand life at home no longer. He moved out of the family home permanently and went to live with the Peningtons, looking upon Isaac and Mary as his parents. By now, they had three sons and Tom became their tutor.

At this time the persecution of the Quakers was at its height and both Isaac and Tom spent time intermittently in Aylesbury Gaol, but this did not stop Tom enjoying his new found circle of friends. At one of their meetings, held at Coleshill, a windswept hamlet high on the hill above Amersham, he met a girl. Her name was Mary Ellis. He helped her in many ways, never dreaming for one moment that she was falling in love with him. She from the first admired his gentle ways and considerate manner, but felt she had no chance at all with him as he was constantly in the company of the beautiful Guli.

Guli was much admired and had droves of suitors, eligible young men from all walks of life, but the countryside began to buzz with talk that she and Tom were to be betrothed. Some of these suitors, eaten up with jealousy, went so far as to say spiteful things of Tom to Isaac and Mary Penington, hinting that Tom had only become a Quaker in order to marry Guli. This shaft really went home with Tom and, in his autobiography, he strongly refuted this and pointed out that he went through much pain to become a Quaker and lost his entire family and inheritance in the process. But he does not reveal in so many words exactly how he felt about Guli, only to say: 'I was ignorant of the various fears which filled the jealous heads of some concerning me, neither was I so stupid nor so divested of all humanity as not to be sensible of the real and innate worth and virtue which adorned that excellent dame, and attracted the eyes and hearts of so many'.

Why did their romance not progress? Was it that Guli looked on Tom only as a dear friend, or was it that Tom, disinherited by his father, felt he had nothing to offer her? Or then again, was it because Guli had already met 'the one for whom she was reserved.'? Whatever it was, Tom goes on to say, not without humour, 'I resolved to shun the rock on which I had seen so many run and split.'

It was around this time that Guli's parents asked Tom to accompany her on a journey to her Uncle Springett's in Sussex. The two young Quakers set off on horseback with Guli's servant, John Gigger, in attendance.

On their return Tom walked to Coleshill, where he tapped on the door of the lodgings of Mary Ellis, who was recovering from an illness. Tom first began with polite enquiries about her health and the weather, but before he knew where he was, he found himself proposing to her. She was astonished, Tom later admitted, 'for she had taken the aprehension, as others also had, that mine eye had been fixed elsewhere and nearer home.'

After a respectable time of courtship, Tom and Mary were married in a Friend's house on 28th October, 1669. They lived in a cottage at Hunger Hill, Coleshill, for the rest of their lives.

Meanwhile, 'the one for whom Guli was reserved' had turned up in the shape of the dashing William Penn. Exactly when their first meeting took place is not known, but Penn visited Bury Farm at Amersham for solace from the Peningtons on the very day his father turned him out of the house for being a Quaker – a similar story to that of Tom.

The man who later founded Pennsylvania was a most handsome fellow with a decided air about him. There was instant mutual attraction between Guli and himself and every moment he could spare he spent at Bury Farm. Two years elapsed between the time they met and the time they were affianced. During this time, Penn suffered persecution along with his fellow Quakers. For example, in 1671 Penn arrived at the Quaker Meeting House in Gracechurch Street, London, to find it closed and guarded by soldiers, so he addressed those gathering outside. He was arrested and charged that 'with force of arms he did assemble to the disturbance of the peace'. Although the jury found that Penn was guilty only of preaching and speaking, the Mayor, who sat on the Bench, refused to let them be dismissed until they came up with the verdict he wanted. Thanks to the courage of the jury Penn was found not guilty, but was still fined and imprisoned. He wrote to Guli from prison that on his return they would never again be parted. He kept his promise for on 6th March 1672, they were married, and the entry on the register is in the unmistakable handwriting of their loving friend, Tom Ellwood. He and his wife, Mary, were there at the ceremony, as was Mary Penington and her children, but not so poor Isaac who was once again in prison.

In that spring, when the woods and hedgerows burst into life, none could have been happier than the two couples who remained loving friends for the rest of their lives. Even now they are together, for a visit to the peaceful Friends Meeting House at Jordans will show four little headstones resting close together – Tom and Mary, William and Guli.

The
Black Canons

WHEN the life of William de Missenden was miraculously saved from a shipwreck, he was filled with gratitude, and looked around for some way in which he could show his appreciation. What better way, he thought, than to provide for good and holy men to serve God and humanity in meekness and humility through the centuries to come, within the pleasant confines of a building of character.

In his imagination he could see it all – an Abbey, standing beneath the shelter of a lofty eminence in the Chiltern Hills, supplied with water from the river Misbourne flowing through the valley, the beechwoods providing fuel and feed for pigs. He could just see those holy men settled in a peaceful life pattern sitting at the windows copying manuscripts, hoeing the gardens on the hillside, some going out into the surrounding villages to act as parish priests and tend their flocks. On the main route to London, the Abbey could provide weary travellers with a welcome and repose that they would be loath to leave.

And so it was that Missenden Abbey came to be founded in 1133, and it grew to become one of the largest and wealthiest in England. More than one landowner was only too pleased to donate some of his extensive lands and estates to the Abbey in order to keep on the right side of heaven. Robert de Sifrewast went so far as to make over 'to the Canons of Missenden Abbey my man Wuluric the Miller' for the sum of five shillings. The monks, wearing black habits, literally dominated the surrounding area and became known as the Black Canons.

The dream of William de Missenden had to all intents and purposes come true. But how would he have felt could he have foreseen that through the coming centuries up until its dissolution in 1538, the records and chronicles of the Abbey would not always show peace and piety in his dreamed-of Utopia.

The Abbey came under the jurisdiction of the Bishop of Lincoln and every so often he sent a representative to inspect, receive complaints and report back to him. A list was then drawn up of injunctions and improvements not only to the buildings but to the Canons themselves.

As early as 1236, the Abbot was dismissed after such a visitation and, in 1297, a novice cut his throat for fear of discipline, which would seem to indicate a slight feeling of guilt about something. Neither did the Bishop appreciate prescriptions for certain diseases drawn up by the monks which included 'oil of black snails' and the 'marrow of horse-bones'.

For over a century all seemed peaceful, until 1433, when it was reported that the Bishop's representative was unhappy about the behaviour of the inmates of the Abbey. Immediately after his visit the Abbot received a list of injunctions and was told in no uncertain terms to exhort his Canons forthwith to tighten their discipline.

Some years later there began the great dispute or wrangle between the Abbots Robert Risborough and Henry Honour. In 1462, Risborough, whilst in office, could not have been on the friendliest of terms with his colleagues for he suddenly felt it necessary to appeal to the King for protection against them. The outcome was that they were summoned to indemnify him against injury or damage to his property.

Only a month later, he was abruptly dismissed from office and declared guilty of simony (misuse of ecclesiastical preferment). His place was taken by Henry Honour who reigned in comparative peace and seemed to be a man true to his name, of honesty and respect. One would think that was the end of it, but no. Seven years later, Risborough challenged the position of Henry Honour and this time appealed to Thomas Rotherham, Chancellor of the Realm, who surprisingly threw the unfortunate Henry Honour into the Fleet Prison and re-instated Risborough.

It became obvious that a miscarriage of justice had been performed, for when Thomas Rotherham later became Bishop of Lincoln and consequently in a better position to become acquainted with the goings on at Missenden Abbey, Risborough took fright and resigned, taking up the living at Kimble. Poor Henry Honour, after spending some three years in prison, was released and returned to the Abbey as Abbot.

Robert Risborough however just could not let things be and, a few years later from his Kimble home, once again complained to the King that he had been wrongly deposed. Although a writ was issued for his restoration, by this time, Thomas Rotherham was not having the wool pulled over his eyes again and he conducted a thorough investigation. Henry Honour was confirmed in his position and there he stayed.

It was in 1518 that Bishop William Attwater came on the scene and arrived at the Abbey to conduct yet another enquiry. He considered himself a fair-minded man and decreed that the Abbot and all the Canons should be examined and each one allowed to make complaints. He may well have regretted this since he was deluged with them. As a result, John Johns was declared detrimental to the community at large and ordered to perform his tasks in a proper manner. The language of the butler left a lot to be desired and both he and the rest of the servants were commanded not to abuse the Canons, however justified, and to regulate their own behaviour.

The most scandalous and troublesome reports appeared on the Bishop's desk some twelve years later. Shaken to the core, he immediately sent a representative to the Abbey to really sort things out. At that time, including the Abbot and the servants, there were approximately fifty persons residing there. The Canons were asked to give reports. All but one gave the usual string of complaints. John Slythurst was the exception, which was not surprising, as he was the subject of most of the other complaints and was described as being a 'sower of dissension' and was also guilty of pederasty. Furthermore, he had shown criminal tendencies by making a duplicate set of keys in order to facilitate ease of movement to and from the village at night. He was confined to his cell.

Despite this, things cannot have improved overmuch, as the following year the Bishop himself made a trip to the Abbey, principally to look into the reports he had received on the behaviour of the Abbot and Canon Roger Palmer with a certain lady of the village. The Abbot crumbled immediately and confessed to having had an improper relationship with her both before and after her marriage. Roger Palmer's association with her was declared to be an outright scandal, as he had been seen leaving the lady's abode 'in his doblett and jerkyn and with his sword at his side'. The Abbot was suspended and Palmer 'gated', and forbidden office in the community. The Bishop was, to say the least, scathing in his remarks. The slackness of discipline was said to be appalling and some rather sober-sided people were put in charge with orders that no woman was to be allowed near the Abbey.

At the Dissolution of the Monasteries by Henry VIII, there were many who thought that if any deserved it, Missenden did. It must be remembered though that it is scandalous behaviour that makes news, and of those Canons who must have lived good and gentle lives in service to others, little is recorded.

The last Abbot, John Ottwell, surrendered the Abbey upon receipt of the most generous pension of £50 per year. It is interesting to note that, when he died in 1558, he left a wife and family. Canon Thomas Bernard became the Vicar of Great Missenden and John Slythurst of ill fame became the Vicar of The Lee, but as he did not fulfil requirements and did not subsequently serve The Lee, his pension was reduced. As for the amorous Roger Palmer, he too collected an annual pension and disappeared, perhaps to a certain house in the village.

The House
the Baron Built

ONE fine day in the late 19th century Baron Ferdinand de
Rothschild, out hunting, rode up to the crest of Lodge
Hill at Waddesdon, some 490 feet above sea level, and became
entranced by the panoramic view of several counties spread
out before him. At that time he was anxious to acquire a home
for himself and the estate of Waddesdon and Winchendon was
up for sale at the time. It consisted of some 2,700 acres, all
farmland but with no house or park. But that matchless view
won the day with Baron Ferdinand, and he purchased the
estate from the Duke of Marlborough in 1874 and planned to
build his own residence of size on Lodge Hill as soon as
possible.

Touring France some years before, he had admired the
chateaux of the Valois and ever since had nursed a strong
desire to build something on the same lines. He selected a
French architect by the name of Destailleur, who was considered the absolute top in his profession and a French landscape designer, M. Laine, to create the roads, terraces, gardens and plantations.

After many discussions the work commenced. Laying the
foundations was not an easy task. The steep hill needed
digging and levelling and there were roads to be laid out.
Local labour was employed as much as possible, but was
supplemented by a gang of outside navvies when necessary.
The new Manor needed water which had to be brought from

Aylesbury. Seven miles of pipe were laid, first to the village and then the extra miles to the house, at great cost to the Baron, and of much benefit to the farms and villages it passed through on the way.

The Bath stone with which the house was built was transported to the site by means of a special steam tram from the railway. All other materials were brought by road. The land around the Manor was bereft of woods which it was feared would give it a very bleak setting. Trees were needed, not just young ones that take a long time to grow, but some that were mature. To the wonder and astonishment of the surrounding countryside, the Baron gave orders that oak and elm and other trees of maturity, some over forty feet high be brought and planted in groups and avenues. These trees were dug up with as much of their original earth as possible still clinging to the roots and special carts had to be made to carry them. Percheron mares were imported from Normandy to pull the heavy loads and it sometimes took sixteen of them to do so. Telegraph poles and wires had to be temporarily moved to one side to let them through.

A few years before in Paris, many of the old houses of the French aristocracy had been demolished so as to make way for the long straight boulevards we see today and the Baron bought up as much as he could of their splendid panelling offered for sale. This now enhances the treasure trove of pictures and furniture at Waddesdon.

By the time he had finished, the Baron had built himself one of the most splendid houses in England, if not in Europe. He first slept in his house in 1883 and held a grand housewarming almost immediately afterwards. His close friend, the Prince of Wales, was among the first to stay at Waddesdon and became a frequent and regular guest.

Meanwhile, the village of Waddesdon had taken on a new lease of life with a new village hall, hotel, reading room and many fine new cottages, yet still managing to retain its old world charm.

Soon everybody that was anybody wanted an invitation to

stay at Waddesdon Manor and distinguished guests were streaming through the lodge gates. Stories going back to Windsor must have excited the curiosity of Queen Victoria who announced to the Baron whilst dining at the Castle, that she proposed to honour him with her presence at Waddesdon. Eventually the visit was fixed for 14th May, 1890. The Baron was flattered and so was Buckinghamshire. The Queen had never, since her succession, visited that part of the county and the people were bursting with loyalty and excitement. The town of Aylesbury with its population of 9,000, was beside itself and lashed out £300 for stands, decorations, banners and flags which blossomed in profusion as the great day came nearer. Waddesdon was close behind and even this small village had a stand for the Baron's tenants and villagers to obtain a good view of the diminutive Queen.

Much preparation and scuttling here and there was going on at the Manor with the Baron perpetually locked in communication with Sir Henry Ponsonby and Princess Louise, the Queen's daughter, so that all would go smoothly with the Royal visit. On the preceding day, 13th May, the Queen's small pony and carriage arrived to be ready to carry her around the estate.

The morning of 14th May dawned, perfect and sunny with just a light cool breeze. The Baron reached Aylesbury Station to find his cousin, Lord Rothschild, pacing up and down the platform ready to receive the Queen and perform his first official function as Lord Lieutenant of the County.

A hiss of steam and the Royal train glided majestically into the station and the procession to Waddesdon wound its way just as slowly and regally through the County town. The Queen's carriage led the way with numerous others following behind. The route was lined with people who cheered their heads off along the six miles to Waddesdon. The Baron in his carriage put on a spurt so as to be at the Manor to receive his Royal guest and, by some miracle, he stood on the steps ready with his sister, Miss Alice, Princess Louise and members of his family.

The Queen was determined to inspect all the grounds and was taken to the Aviary in her pony carriage. The pony was a cute little fellow, but the parrots and macaws thought otherwise, and screamed and shrieked at him to such an alarming degree that he shied and the visit to the Aviary was cut short. Her Majesty then carried out the usual tree planting ceremony and passed on to be charmed by the glasshouses filled with flowering shrubs, where a bouquet was presented to her. She took tea in the specially erected oriental tent on the lawn in front of the house and it seemed the day had flown as the procession wound its way back to Aylesbury Station. A quick kiss of a tiny hand, which afterwards fluttered from a carriage window and all was over. The Baron was well pleased that everything had gone so well and was extremely flattered that the Queen of England, after so many drab years in retirement, should emerge to see his Waddesdon.

The Baron, M.P. for Aylesbury and Member of the Bucks County Council, died in 1898 and the flag flew at half mast from the Council Offices in Aylesbury. At his death, Waddesdon passed to his sister, Miss Alice, who proved a skilful custodian, and from her to James de Rothschild, who in turn bequeathed it to the National Trust, so that everyone could visit and view this wonderful building and the collections inside.

It has been said that Buckinghamshire was fortunate indeed in being the county selected as home by the famous Rothschild family, who brought with them prosperity, generosity, and a record of service to the community—and left behind matchless treasures.

The
Pretty Box

In the village of Chalfont St Giles there stands a quaint little cottage set in a fragrant and well-tended garden. It has a low ceiling, lattice windows and a tall chimney. In this atmosphere it is easy to imagine John Milton sitting by the open fire musing on his writings, or being read to by his clever daughter, Deborah. For it is here, in this cottage, that he lived from May 1665 to April 1666. The plague was raging in London and he, like many other city dwellers, feared for his family. He wrote to his old pupil and reader, Thomas Ellwood, the Quaker, asking him to find a place for him to live in the area. Ellwood was only too pleased to be of service. The two men he respected most in life were John Milton and Isaac Penington.

He excitedly wrote it all down at the time: 'I was desired by my quondam master, Milton, to take a house for him in the neighbourhood where I dwelt, that he might go out of the city for the safety of himself and his family, the pestilence then growing hot in London. I took a pretty box for him at Giles Chalfont. . . .'

Ellwood then wrote to tell Milton that he had found the ideal place with a garden, which was a must as far as Milton was concerned. All was set for the poet to come and Tom could hardly wait to welcome him, when a most unfortunate incident occurred.

Tom Ellwood and Isaac Penington attended a funeral at nearby Amersham. The deceased was one Edward Perot, a resident of that town and a most respected Quaker, though with a rather unusual turn of mind. Quaker Perot, some years before, being extremely fervent in his belief, decided to go straight to the heart of the matter. He had travelled to Rome and tried to convert the Pope. History shows that his powers of persuasion were not successful, but it would be interesting to know what kind of a reception he received. Be that as it may, he had been a well-liked man and a good percentage of the Quakers from a wide area were expected to attend his funeral, which was arranged to be held on 1st May 1665 at Amersham. Mr Perot had specifically asked to be buried in an orchard he owned at the other end of the town from his house, which meant that the cortege would wend its way the length of the town.

It so happened that early on that morning, the 1st May, a certain Ambrose Bennett of Bullstrodes, a barrister at law, Justice of the Peace and a detester of all Quakers without exception, was riding through Amersham. Hearing that a Quaker funeral was expected to take place in the town later that same day, he and his men repaired to the comforts of the *Griffin Inn*, where drinking and joking with their feet up on the table, they waited for the funeral to pass by.

The coffin was taken up and borne upon the shoulders of Quaker Friends along the street, followed by mourners Thomas Ellwood, Isaac Penington, Morgan Watkins and many others. Little did they know what was awaiting them at the *Griffin*.

As the procession drew level with the Inn, out rushed Ambrose Bennett, supported by constables and 'a rabble of rude fellows'. Bennett struck the foremost bearer an almighty slap with his sword, commanding that the coffin should be set down. The man refused to do so. This sent Mr Bennett into such a fit of rage that he seized upon the coffin, tore it from the shoulders of the bearers so that it fell to the ground with a crash, and there it stayed. The remainder of those taking part in the procession were dragged into the *Griffin* and placed under guard. Ten were picked out, Isaac and Tom among them, and committed to Aylesbury Gaol.

Meanwhile, the coffin and body of the unfortunate Edward Perot lay in the road, no-one daring to touch it, and all travellers that passed by – horsemen, coaches, carts or wagons – were forced to go around it. At last, a grumbling grave-digger was called upon to dig a grave in the unconsecrated part of the churchyard for poor Quaker Perot, who was buried without ceremony, much to the distress of his widow.

Isaac and Tom were released in a month, but all this time Tom had worried about John Milton arriving at Chalfont St Giles. With Isaac and himself in prison, there were no friends there to meet and welcome him. Even Milton's old friend, Colonel George Fleetwood of the Vache, was abroad in exile.

Immediately Tom arrived home, he set off for the 'pretty box' at Chalfont to greet his friend. After the usual greetings and conversation, Milton handed Tom a manuscript and told him to take it home, read it at his leisure and let him know his opinion of it. Tom's wonder grew as he read it. He knew it was a poem of outstanding excellence – it was called *Paradise Lost*. When Tom took it back, Milton eagerly asked how he liked it. Tom told him, but added that as he had written of Paradise Lost, what had he to say about Paradise Found?

Milton said nothing, was silent for a while and then spoke upon another subject.

Whilst Milton lived at Chalfont, 14,000 people died of the plague in London. By 1666 it had begun to wane, but had reached Chalfont with one or two cases recorded there. There seemed little reason to stay. He and his family had lived in the cottage throughout the winter and they went back in early spring.

Some time later, Tom Ellwood on one of his visits to London, visited Milton at his London home, which he seldom failed to do when he was in the City. Tom records that Milton then showed him a second poem he had written entitled *Paradise Regained* and said to Tom in a very pleasant voice, 'This is owing to you, for you put it in my head by what you said at Chalfont.'

Poachers and Keepers

THE poaching of game has been happening ever since one man owned land and another did not, and, through the centuries, penalties and punishments have ranged from fines and mutilation to imprisonment, transportation and death.

Times were often hard for villagers and men were frequently driven to poach in order to keep their families fed. The Rev J. E. Linnell writing in 1932 tells the story of two poachers. In 1748, Stowe Park was teeming with deer and presented a great temptation to two local men, Joe Adams and Jim Tyrell, who ventured forth to secure the meat they needed. They moved carefully and stealthily through the moonlit park to avoid keepers. At last they spotted their quarry, a group of deer. A quick chase brought down a buck. It was a heavy burden and, as they set off carrying their kill along the way they had come, they ran slap into an ambush of keepers. Joe and Jim put up strong resistance, but they were overpowered and led off first to Stowe House and then to the County Gaol.

Back in the village, the wives of the two men awaited their return. Mary Adams, only recently married to Joe, stepped outside her cottage door, listening eagerly for his step and longing to see his figure coming down the lane. As the dawn of another day broke, her worst fears were realised. A messenger from Stowe came to tell the village that Joe and Jim had been caught stealing park deer.

73

Mary and the wife of Jim Tyrell set off to plead with old Lord Cobham, the owner of Stowe House, for surely the fate of their two husbands lay completely in his hands. He agreed to see them and showed a certain sympathy as they implored him to use his influence to save their men. He promised faithfully that he would have them home on a certain day in the following week and the two women returned vastly relieved. When the day specified arrived, a cart carrying two coffins arrived at the door of Mary Adams and the driver delivered the message from Lord Cobham. They would kindly note that he had kept his word!

Despite such tragic results as this, poaching continued, sometimes for the sheer thrill of it, the adventure and excitement of creeping through the woods under the very noses of the keepers. A battle of wits existed between a poacher called Harry Wright and gamekeeper John Wilkins of Chesham. It seems quite certain from Wilkins' autobiography published in 1892 that these two men had a healthy respect or even a liking for one another. Harry was a wily chap and made poaching a paying game. He used his brains and had never been caught red-handed. He was particularly fond of taking eggs from pheasants nests and Wilkins decided to be as crafty as Harry. He bribed a friend to tell Harry of the exact location of a pheasant's nest under a certain hedge, then he made the nest himself and filled it with rotten eggs.

Wilkins lay in wait, hidden in a thicket near the nest, and just as he had hoped, along came Harry and furtively helped himself to all the eggs, putting them in the pockets of his jacket. Wilkins walked around so as to meet him, as if the two men had met by chance in the wood. 'Good mornin', John' – 'Good mornin', Harry'. Harry was very pleased with himself and looked as if he was inwardly laughing at the keeper, until Wilkins remarked that he understood Harry was very partial to the odd pheasant egg, whereupon Harry's face changed and he angrily asked what Wilkins meant. Wilkins said 'Come on, Harry' and quickly struck the pockets of Harry's jacket an almightly slap and the rotten eggs, giving off a ghastly, pungent smell, ran in a gooey mass down poor Harry's trousers. Back in the town for years afterwards Harry was ribbed by people asking him if he had enjoyed the breakfast of rotten eggs given to him by Keeper John Wilkins. No doubt Harry took his revenge at a later date.

Alas, this kind of fun between keeper and poacher did not often exist. A young boy from Horwood was charged with taking pheasants eggs and sentenced to one month imprisonment, as well as entering into recognizances to keep the peace for the term of his natural life.

Under the Enclosure Acts, the landowners had been given opportunities to enlarge their parks by taking into them some of the common lands, where the labourer had always been free to take game. The villagers felt robbed and that the game still belonged to everyone. It was hard for a man with a growing family, living on a few shillings a week, to see rabbit and hare dinners running around the outskirts of his village and to be prohibited from touching them. The local poacher was, therefore, looked upon as a hero, not only because he more often than not made fools of the keepers, who they regarded as villains of the piece, but also to some extent it seemed a way of getting back at the landowner. But this local poacher was not to be confused with the gangs of professional poachers who came from the cities in organised force to steal the game and supply the urban markets. As they invaded the countryside, so the keepers armed themselves in bands, and the affrays that followed have been named by historians the 'Poaching Wars'. Of this kind of poacher, Thomas Hood wrote:

> 'No county from his tricks are safe,
> In each he tried his lucks;
> And when the Keepers were in Beds
> He often was in Bucks'.

In 1825, two of these city poachers named Lynn and Hogg came down from Lambeth and visited Whaddon Chase in the hope of taking some illicit game back to town. They waited for night to fall in a local hostelry and imbibed an excessive quantity of liquor, especially Lynn. As they crept through the woods of Whaddon Chase, they became separated, Lynn going on in front. He moved through the bracken for some way before he became aware of following footsteps. He paused and stood stock still. There it was again – a keeper without a doubt. Lynn moved behind a clump of bushes and waited. A shadowy figure emerged from the trees and Lynn, with the butt end of his gun, struck it a tremendous blow on the head. Imagine his feelings when he discovered that he had killed outright, not a keeper but his friend, Hogg. He was arrested and tried at Aylesbury but, pleading that he was affected by delirium tremens and mistook Hogg for a keeper, a verdict was returned of 'guilty but insane'. Perhaps the verdict would have been different had it been a keeper that was killed.

The Government had strengthened the Game Laws to the extent that anyone now found with a net was liable to seven years' imprisonment, and this caused much trouble. In north Buckinghamshire, a local man called Eborn had been seen by a 'watcher' to pick up a snare. It was empty and Eborn denied that it was his. He was a good, honest working man with no previous convictions whatsoever. He had long been out of work and his wife and family were half starved, yet he was sentenced to 32 weeks in the County Gaol. Both the *Aylesbury News* and the national *Times* spotlighted this case as an argument against the Game Laws and Sir Harry Verney of Claydon House, Member of Parliament for Buckingham, was also stirred into righteous action. He pointed out to the Buckingham Quarter Sessions at Aylesbury how very scandalous this case was and put a motion to them 'that the preservation of Game in such large abundance was causing the inhabitants of the County nothing but injury.' He also drew their attention to the plight of the tenant farmers who were not allowed to defend their crops by killing the landowner's game, and he reminded them that there were some parts of the county where a quarter of the crop was destroyed by game. The motion was lost and later that year in the last week of

October and first week of November, in Buckinghamshire alone, 26 poachers were sent to prison.

Buckinghamshire is still proud of a farmer called Harris who was not a tenant and owned his own land. The Earl of Buckinghamshire refused to pay damages for the destruction done by his game to Harris' crops. Harris did no more than invite all the sportsmen for miles around to a shoot on his land; at the same time he made it known that no poacher need fear prosecution for poaching on his ground and that the Earl's gamekeepers would be prosecuted for trespass if they tried to interfere. The hares and pheasants were disposed of in their thousands, much to the displeasure of the Earl. Whilst he had gone to endless trouble and expense to preserve such game, Harris and others had had both the profit and the fun.

The bad reputation of the keepers was not generally without foundation. Some were known to set out in gangs to deliberately inflict bodily harm on poachers, and violence was commonplace. In 1837, a man named Bates was convicted of the murder of a keeper, although he pleaded self-defence, and sentenced to die without mercy. Gibbs, in his records of the county, notes '31st March – the man Bates was hanged this morning on the new drop in front of Aylesbury Gaol, a victim of the Game Laws. Comparatively few spectators were present. People are becoming tired of this hanging.'

J. K. Fowler, sitting in the gardens of Hughenden with Benjamin Disraeli, talked of the grievances brought about by the Game Laws, and the great man said that if he had his way he would soon settle the question. When 'J.K.' asked him how, he replied 'Abolish gamekeepers.'

The
Standard-Bearer

SIR Edmund Verney, Standard-Bearer to King Charles I, was killed at the battle of Edgehill in 1642, and his ghost is said to haunt the top floors of Claydon House looking for his lost hand. And thereby hangs one of the most touching stories of loyalty in history.

Edmund Verney was born in Drury Lane in 1590. His father, old Sir Edmund, died at The Stone, Chalfont St Giles in 1599. This left his nine year old son to be brought up solely by his mother, Dame Mary, a highly intelligent woman. To her must go the credit for the shaping of his excellent character for he grew into a chivalrous, kind and honourable gentleman and became close friends with Prince Henry, the eldest son of James I.

Unfortunately, at 18 years old, Prince Henry was suddenly smitten with a strange illness. He went rapidly into decline and died within six weeks. All England mourned their favourite Prince and Edmund was to say later that nothing in his early life caused him so much grief as did the death of his friend.

Edmund came of age in 1611 and was immediately knighted and placed in the household of Prince Charles, who, after the death of his elder brother, became heir to the throne. Charles' character was just the opposite to that of his late brother, Henry. He was an introvert, studious and sensitive. Despite the fact that he was ten years Edmund's junior, the two became friends and it was the beginning of a life-long relationship.

The estates of Claydon in Buckinghamshire had been in the Verney family for a considerable number of years, although leased to the Giffard family. Just over the hill was Hillesden, where lived Margaret Denton, the daughter of Sir Thomas Denton. Sir Edmund and she fell in love and married when he was 22 and she 18. It proved to be a long and happy marriage, she being of a gentle and loving disposition and an exemplary wife. They lived for a while at Hillesden until they could move into Claydon. Over the years they had twelve children.

On the death of King James I, Charles became King and appointed his friend Sir Edmund Verney Standard-Bearer and Knight Marshall. But something untoward was going on in the country – there were murmurings from Parliament – names like Pym, Hampden and Cromwell were coming very much to the fore. Sir Edmund foresaw trouble and when John Hampden made his stand against the Ship Money levied by Charles, he felt a terrible foreboding. He knew there would be strife if the King did not change his ways and he hoped desperately that Charles would not remain obstinately blind to the desires of honourable Parliamentarians.

Adding to his concern was the fact that he and Lady Verney now had grown-up sons. The eldest, Ralph, defended the Parliamentary cause. The third son, Edmund ('Mun') would undoubtedly go with the Royalist side if there was a clash. Sir Edmund could not bear to think of his family divided, let alone his country. What is more, his mind was in turmoil with regard to his own position, of which he said 'For my part, I do not like the quarrel, and do heartily wish the King would yield and consent to what they desire, so that my conscience is only concerned in honour and in gratitude to serve my Master. I have eaten his bread and served him near thirty years, and will not forsake him, and choose rather to lose my life (which I am sure I shall do) to preserve and defend my conscience.'

In that October of 1642, neither the Royalist nor the

Parliamentarian Armies were very good at scouting and on the 22nd of that month, Quartermasters from both sides were out looking for billets when they suddenly came upon one another at Kineton. This frightened the life out of both parties and they rushed back to their respective armies.

The next morning it was revealed that, under cover of darkness, the Royalists had taken up a most advantageous position on the top of Edgehill. The two armies sat and looked at one another. After a time, it became all too apparent that the Parliamentarians were not going to be fools enough to attack up the hill – so the Royalists came down.

It was a cold, bright morning and, just before the battle commenced, Sir Edmund breakfasted with his old friend, the King. It was to be their last meeting. The Parliamentary Army opened fire first and King Charles himself ignited the charge for the Royalist guns to answer. The dashing Prince Rupert, as impetuous as ever, rushed down the slope with his cavalry and attacked a portion of the enemy, breaking through and putting them to flight. He then went on to make the great mistake of giving chase, thus leaving the King's troops to stand against the Roundheads from another direction. The struggle around the King's Standard was fast and furious, and it became obvious that the Royalists could not withstand the onslaught.

The Roundheads called out and offered Sir Edmund his life if he would hand over the King's Standard. He called back that his life was his own but that the Standard belonged to his Sovereign and he would not surrender it while he lived. They took him at his word and rushed him. Sixteen of them fell by his sword before he disappeared under a mêlée of fighting men. A Roundhead emerged carrying the Standard – around the staff still clung the hand of the Standard-Bearer who had grasped it. Sir Edmund had been faithful to the death. On one of the fingers of the hand was a ring given to him by the King. His body was never found.

So died one of the most gallant gentlemen in English history who, it is said, still looks for his missing hand at Claydon House.

The
Miser's Bequest

JOHN Camden Neild made Ebenezer Scrooge seem like the last of the big spenders. Born in 1780 and owning considerable lands and property in Buckinghamshire, he was miserly in the extreme. His sole preoccupation was in finding ways to extract and make money – and then, how to save it. The only avenue to any emotion in this gentleman was via his pocket.

He certainly had not inherited his parsimonious spirit from his father, James Neild, a Sheriff of Buckinghamshire. He was well known for his philanthropy, who liberally gave of his time and money in the service of the community. Neither had it come from his maternal grandfather, William Camden, the famous antiquary to whom the county is indebted for his early *History of Buckinghamshire*. Exactly how, when and where this disproportionate love of money reared its ugly head in John is not known. He had received a good education, ending up at Cambridge, and was called to the Bar. He was only 34 when he came into his father's estates worth £250,000, and it was hoped all round the county that he would follow in his generous parent's footsteps. But no! His habits and appearance became even more peculiar and his inherent meanness only too apparent.

Anyone who had occasion to be walking along one of Buckinghamshire's many lanes or highways, in the early part of the last century, may well have beheld the strange figure of John Camden Neild coming towards him with jerky though

trim gait, perchance on his way to one of his many farms to collect the rent – to the last farthing! He would behold a man of no more than five feet in height with an exceptionally large head set upon an extraordinarily short neck, and he would notice that his dress was remarkably shabby, even for those days, with tight brown pantaloons, a threadbare swallow-tailed coat with gilt buttons, over a dirty buff waistcoat topped with a high shirt collar and a large frill. His shoes were of hessian, patched and down at heel and that the whole of this personage was topped with a much worn low-crowned beaver hat. Drawing closer, he would see that the stockings were full of holes and that John Neild was carrying, as he always did, an aged green umbrella (whether this was its original colour or whether it had turned green with mould, who can say!). He would not allow, under any circumstances, his clothes to be brushed or cleaned as he said this destroyed the nap and shortened their life.

He preferred to walk all the way to his estates in Buckinghamshire from his house in Chelsea in order to save the coach fare. However, when he visited his estates in Kent, he was forced to travel by coach, but always rode on the top with the driver as the fare was cheaper. And he was never known to wear a greatcoat, even in the most severe weather. On one occasion in a bitter, driving blizzard of gales and snow, the coach on which he was travelling pulled into an Inn in order that the passengers and the driver might receive vital warmth. As they were enjoying their hot rum punch by a roaring fire, they beheld the figure of John Camden Neild, coatless, and still perched on top of the waiting coach. Thinking the poor man poverty stricken and unable to afford to come inside, they passed around a hat and sent him out a hot rum punch, for which he thanked them politely and had the nerve to drink it down!

Although he was not known to spend a penny on any of his farms, he stayed overnight at them so as to save the expense of staying at an inn. When calling on a tenant at Buckland Common, near Chesham, he gave the farmer's wife all of two pennies to boil him two eggs and buy a penny roll, and these he ate as he walked along the road to Aylesbury to save the cost of stopping for a meal.

Once, just once, he ordered a beef lunch at the *White Hart* at Aylesbury and the waiter, coming unexpectedly into the room, was horrified to see John Camden Neild, a gentleman of good family and property, cutting two more slices off the joint which he carefully laid between two slices of bread and put in his pocket, obviously in anticipation of his next meal. He was promptly asked for an extra shilling which, after remonstrance, he paid.

His equilibrium was seriously disturbed once, when some shares he owned went 'down the drain'. Staying at Rectory Farm, North Marston, at the time, he attempted suicide in one of the outhouses, some said by cutting his throat and others said by hanging. Undoubtedly, it would have been whichever method was the cheaper. But his tenant's wife, who must have been a saintly soul after the treatment she had received from him, saved his life.

At home he slept on bare boards. He had a black cat and a housekeeper and his regard was given in that order. He paid the housekeeper a pittance which was heavily reduced when he was away from home, as he calculated that she did not then do nearly the same amount of work.

Owning property in North Marston, it was his duty to keep the church in a good state of repair. This he did with reluctance and the time came when the roof definitely needed to be renewed, as the wet congregation began to dwindle somewhat alarmingly. At last he agreed to the re-roofing, but not with lead. He instructed that strips of calico should be used as he said this 'would see him out'. What's more, he sat on the roof of the church to make sure the workmen toiled solidly all day.

In fairness to him, it is said that he did contribute £5 towards the building of a school and he once gave £1 to the Sunday School at North Marston. He rashly promised the sum of £300 towards the building of an Infirmary for Buckinghamshire (who knows, perhaps he felt he may need it one day) but changed his mind because he did not like the site that was chosen. And, of course, there is the story that a son of one of his tenants showed academic promise and that John Neild paid for his education. If this is so, it is right out of character and completely ruins his reputation. He definitely found it more blessed to receive than to give and increased the fortune he had inherited from his father to £500,000.

During his life, John Camden Neild brought no warmth whatsoever into the life of anyone and caused no ripple in the tide of human affairs whatsoever, yet when he died in 1852 it was a very different matter, for his death caused a national stir. What earthly reason he had will never be known, but he left his entire fortune to 'her most Gracious Majesty Queen Victoria', who must have been just as stunned as everyone else.

He died at his house in Chelsea and was buried in the chancel of North Marston Church. Many people attended the funeral but they came to watch, not to grieve. His tenants and workmen were there, but there was no tear from them, as they thought any change in landlord could only be for the better. One old villager was heard to remark 'Poor chap – if he knew how much it cost to bring 'im 'ere, he would have come down 'ere to die.'

On proof of the will, Queen Victoria increased many of the bequests and made provision for the housekeeper for the rest of her life. She also secured an annuity on the farmer's wife who had saved the life of Mr Neild. She caused the strips of calico on the roof of North Marston Church to be replaced with lead and restored the chancel, at the same time inserting a stained glass window as a memorial to John Camden Neild. Then, it is said, and only then, she went on to purchase Balmoral.

A Haven
for
Prime Ministers

RIGNALL Road, that leads from Great Missenden to Chequers, the Prime Minister's country seat, must be one of
the most distinguished in the country, for along its leafy way
have travelled some of the greatest leaders of the modern
world, statesmen of distinction and many a crowned head.
Burdens of state must often have slipped away as they gazed
from a limousine at the Chiltern countryside of rolling beechwoods and scattered farms, at last to glide up to the impressive
gates of Chequers.

In 1921 Lord Lee of Fareham handed the house and lands
over to the nation. It was a generous and unselfish gesture.
Both he and Lady Lee had spent a great deal of money on
improvements and restoration and had become very fond of
their home. In the deed of settlement, Lord Lee made his
views clear:

'the better the health of our rulers the more sanely they will
rule, and the inducement to spend two days a week in the high
and pure air of the Chiltern Hills and woods will, it is hoped,
benefit the nation as well as its chosen leaders. The main
features of this scheme are, therefore, designed not merely to

make Chequers available as the official country residence of the Prime Minister of the day, but to tempt him to visit it regularly and to make possible for him to live there, even though his income should be limited to his salary.'

This sentiment was not welcomed by all. At least one Member of the House of Lords felt strongly that Prime Ministers should be available in London seven days a week and was completely unmoved as to whether they had a rest or not.

The early history of the house had been interesting enough – it was mentioned in the Domesday Book of 1086. But it was during Tudor times, when the Hawtrey family were in owner-ship, that the most romantic of stories in connection with Chequers came about.

Lady Mary Grey was cousin to Queen Elizabeth I and also sister to the ill-fated Lady Jane Grey. She fell in love and married, against the Queen's wishes, a Sergeant Porter to the Royal Household by the name of Thomas Keyes. The Queen was not at all pleased as she felt her cousin had married beneath her, which must have been physically difficult to perceive as Lady Mary was of so small a stature as to be considered a dwarf and Tom Keyes was over six feet tall.

The bridegroom was thrown without ceremony into the Fleet prison and William Hawtrey was asked to keep Lady Mary in custody at Chequers where he received strict instruc-tions that she was to talk to no-one with the exception of himself and his wife, neither was she to go out, except when it was necessary for her health that she should take the air.

Poor Lady Mary was for two years locked up in a room at the top of the house. When at last she was released, she was relentlessly kept apart from her husband. He was also released from prison, but died shortly afterwards.

The house then passed through the hands of numerous owners and it was perhaps prophetic that at one time the young Benjamin Disraeli, in the future to become one of England's greatest Prime Ministers, showed interest in purchasing it. He knew the Chilterns well, spending his early life at Bradenham. It seemed he just could not afford Chequers, as he 'cried off' and purchased Hughenden Manor not too far away.

After the donation of the estate to the nation by Lord Lee, Prime Minister Lloyd George was the first to make good use of Chequers as a restful resort, and it was at his invitation that the first notables sped along Rignall Road. They included the French Prime Minister of the time and the Crown Prince of Japan. In fact, Lloyd George and his family so enjoyed staying there that when he resigned as Prime Minister in 1922, the only remark his daughter Megan could think of making was 'Damn! There goes Chequers!'

Bonar Law, the next in office, not only disliked Lord Lee but also the countryside at large and so he firmly declined to use Chequers at all, but Stanley Baldwin loved the English countryside and became thoroughly involved in local activities and events, even going so far as to umpire many a cricket match.

Ramsay MacDonald was a gardener at heart and while spending restful weekends, would sometimes give vent to his frustrations by weeding and digging and, if under pressure, wielding an axe or scythe. He loved Chequers and its history and called it 'a house of comforting and regenerating rest'. He became so attached to the place that his advisers complained they had great difficulty in prising him away. He it was who made the first radio broadcast from Chequers.

Stanley Baldwin was given another turn after MacDonald. The abdication crisis of 1936 had laid him rather low and he spent much of his time recuperating at Chequers. Neville Chamberlain, of the moustache and umbrella, was a walker and Chequers was just the place to indulge in his favourite pastime. His lean figure was often seen striding over the escarpment, pausing to gaze at the view over the Vale of Aylesbury. After all his efforts for peace, he was a shattered man after he was forced to declare war in 1939. Chequers became his haven and he spent very nearly every weekend there.

When the dynamic Winston Churchill arrived in 1940, it was typical of him that he immediately turned Chequers into a war headquarters. Many were the important meetings held and momentous decisions made there. Here it was that he composed and found the spirit to put into those brilliant rallying speeches he made during the war. He entertained many wartime figures, including Generals Eisenhower and de Gaulle. One of the maids had a very nasty turn one morning when the Russian Minister Molotov was a guest. She was required to go to his room with a message and was terrified when faced with the startled Russian waving a gun.

Clement Attlee and his family so fell in love with the house and its surrounding countryside that they acquired Cherry Cottage at Prestwood only a few miles distant.

Anthony Eden was already familiar with Chequers when he came into office as he had visited there as Foreign Secretary in pre-war days. He needed solace after the Suez crisis and found peace there. Shortly afterwards, whilst Harold Macmillan was enjoying Chequers, Konrad Adenauer, the West German Chancellor, was among his many visitors. Odd perhaps to think that only a short time before, Churchill had been conducting a war against the Germans from the very same spot.

There followed Sir Alec Douglas Home and later Harold Wilson, who both enjoyed the tranquillity of the house. Edward Heath felt so exhilarated that he went so far as to play the piano in the Great Hall, and James Callaghan made a national broadcast from there.

Today Mrs Thatcher slips along the roads leading to Chequers. The house has well and truly lived up to the dream Lord Lee envisaged and up to the inscription that appears on the stained-glass window in the ante-room:

'This house of peace and ancient memories was given to England as a thank-offering for her deliverance in the Great War 1914–18 and as a place of rest and recreation for her Prime Ministers for ever.'

And long may it be so!

The
Hell-Fire Club

DR Benjamin Bates of The Manor House, Little Missenden, always said there was nothing in it. Nothing in those scandalous tales of drinking debauchery and orgies amid the ruins of Medmenham Abbey, the meeting place of the Hell-Fire Club. What's more, he continued to say so until his death in 1828 at the rather mellow age of 98. And he should know, being a member of the Club himself, and having made as many trips to Medmenham as the other men of rank and position who kept their frolics and revels to themselves. Furthermore, Dr Bates was personal physician to Sir Francis Dashwood, the founder and leader of the Club.

Sir Francis has been described as an eccentric and, whatever the truth of the Club's 'high jinks', he was certainly that. When he was 16, his father died, and he inherited the title, West Wycombe House and a considerable fortune. The moment he came of age, he travelled to Italy. He fell in love with that sunny, colourful country and it had a profound effect on him for the rest of his life. On his return to England, he and some friends formed the Society of the Dilettanti, a dining Society for gentlemen of wealth and position who had travelled in Italy. Later it devoted itself to patronage of the fine arts. Horace Walpole said that its nominal qualification for membership was not only having been to Italy, but also being drunk. Be that as it may, among its members was a certain

George Knapton, a professional artist, who decided to paint the portraits of his fellow members in 'fancy dress'. He painted Sir Francis Dashwood in the robe of a Franciscan monk (some sort of a pun on his name) gazing at a statue of Venus. It was all a great joke, but it stuck, and they called him St Francis of Wycombe from then on.

Sir Francis became a Member of Parliament in 1741 and married a wealthy widow in 1745. In the same year he founded the 'Brotherhood of Saint Francis of Wycombe', a mock monastic Order. He was determined to find the club its own exclusive premises in Buckinghamshire and his eye fell upon the ruined Abbey at Medmenham. The Abbey had never had a particularly good reputation, as the monks of old had inclined towards lawlessness. Now Francis Duffield was the owner and he was only too happy to lease it to Sir Francis for the express use of the Order of St Francis, which Duffield joined as soon as possible.

Sir Francis had always loved messing about with buildings and he set about restoring and enlarging the Abbey with gusto. The gardens were transformed into breathtaking vistas, with lawns running down to the river and here and there secluded arbours, niches, temples, voluptuous statues, rustic bridges and piers. One area of the park was said to form the shape of a naked woman.

The Brothers of the mock Order used pseudonyms and wore white monks robes, while the prior wore a red bonnet. 'Nuns' were said to be imported from doubtful houses in London, one being a well-known London madam. The early members of the Club were men of learning and fashion, perhaps 'rakes' of the period, but certainly men of status. Among them were such men as Bubb Dodington (Lord Melcombe) a short, fat man of great wit, who gave his fellows much mirth as they watched his ungainly figure chasing the 'nuns' about the gardens. Others included the Earl of Sandwich, Charles Churchill (a former clergyman), the notorious John Wilkes (MP for Aylesbury), William Hogarth (the artist), and Frederick, Prince of Wales, no less.

Paul Whitehead, the satirist and close friend of Sir Francis, was a kind of steward of the Club, keeping the accounts, and making sure the cellar was well stocked. He was possessed of a shocking reputation even before the existence of the Club and his presence in a prominent position could not have enhanced its image. Peeping Toms had a field day at Medmenham watching the 'monks' and 'nuns' cavort and frolic, and stories began to spread in the countryside of even more sinister happenings, of orgies and debauchery, of naked women on altars, obscene rites and even of black magic. There was an inner temple where servants were not allowed. It was even thought that in their rites they managed to invoke the Devil.

Whether or not the genuine article ever appeared is not known, but certainly there was the rather embarrassing story which created a most bitter feud between the Earl of Sandwich and John Wilkes. The latter, practical joker supreme in a Club of practical jokers, dressed up a baboon as the Devil, with horns affixed to its head, and just at the height of the ceremony, let it loose. The shrieking, chattering ape traversed the room at great speed and settled on the shoulder of the Earl of Sandwich, who cringed and screamed in terror 'Spare me, gracious Devil, I am as yet but half a sinner, I have never been so wicked as I intended.' Everyone fell about with laughter and the Earl of Sandwich never forgave Wilkes for making such a fool of him. The two men crossed verbal swords many times through the ensuing years. In the middle of one debate, Sandwich, absolutely infuriated by Wilkes, shouted 'You will die either on the gallows, or of the pox!' To which Wilkes calmly replied: 'That must depend on whether I embrace your lordship's principles or your mistress.'

In the 1750s the people of West Wycombe suffered a succession of harvest failures and, in order to combat unemployment, Sir Francis had built the long, straight main road to High Wycombe. He acquired masses of chalk for the purpose from the caves which already existed in the steep hill at West Wycombe, widening and deepening the caves in the process. On the site of a 5th century Iron Age fort, at the very top of the hill, six hundred feet above the village, he built the Church of St Lawrence. The villagers must have found it arduous and a test of faith to climb the hill to render their devotions every Sunday morning and it would be interesting to know whether the church could boast a good attendance. Some people thought Sir Francis had built the church merely for its pleasing view. John Wilkes said of it 'Some churches have been built for devotion, others for parade or vanity; I believe this is the first church which has been built for a prospect.'

Sir Francis capped the tower of the church with a great golden ball, one hundred feet above the ground, that glistens in the sun. It is a landmark for miles around and looks down the valley to the tower of High Wycombe Church. A quaint pastime of the Buckinghamshire natives is to guess how many men could be seated comfortably inside this ball – some say six, others ten and even twelve. John Wilkes said it was six when describing a drinking orgy with Sir Francis and four others that actually took place inside the ball and he boasted of the amount of drink they consumed. He said later that 'it was the best Globe tavern I was ever in.' Perhaps he wished he had not imbibed so well when he came to use the only exit, which was a rather shaky ladder, and what he thought of the 'prospect' from that angle is a matter of conjecture!

In 1762 Sir Francis was appointed Chancellor of the Exchequer, which astonished most people, including Sir Francis. The Government of Lord Bute was a poor one however and not of long duration, and with it went the Chancellor's post, but not before politics had entered the Club. Some of the members began to talk outside about what went on at Medmenham, and Sir Francis decided to vacate the Abbey and to hold future meetings in the caves at West Wycombe, which would provide greater safety and completely rule out the chances of being overlooked. Here the orgies, drinking and gaming went on as before, and the caverns and passages can be viewed to this day.

Sir Francis died in 1781. The 'Order' he founded was not

given the name of the Hell-Fire Club from its inception, but it seems to have acquired it by sinister and bizarre reputation. Whether the tales connected with it are wholly or even partly true will perhaps never be known. If the truth is that the members were just practical jokers, and history has painted their club in lurid colours they never intended, surely the last joke is on them!

Bibliography

Lipscombe *County of Buckingham*.

J. K. Fowler *Echoes of Old County Life*, *Recollections of Old Country Life*, *Records of Old Times*.

E. Kaye *A History of Missenden Abbey* 1973.

P. Somerset Fry *Chequers* H.M.S.O. 1977.

P. Verney *The Standard Bearer* Hutchinson & Co. 1963.

Harman *Sketches of the Bucks Countryside* Blandford Press Ltd. 1934.

Gibbs *Records and Worthies of Bucks*.

D. McCormick *The Hell-Fire Club* Jarrolds 1958.

H. Hopkins *The Long Affray* Martin Secker and Warburg 1985.

E. G. Walsh *The Poachers Companion* Boydell Press 1984.

Mrs. James de Rothschild *The Rothschilds of Waddesdon* Collins 1979.

Ellwoods Autobiography.

I. Melton *History of the Wotton Railway* London Underground Railway Soc.

C. Hibbert *Disraeli and his World* 1978.

F. Hansford Miller *John Hampden* Shire Publications 1976.

J. Wilkins *The Autobiography of an English Gamekeeper*.